Interactive Distance Learning
Exercises that Really Work!

Turn Classroom Exercises

into Effective and Enjoyable

Distance Learning Activities

Karen Mantyla

ASTD

Ordering information: Books published by the American Society for Training & Development can be ordered by calling 800.628.2783 or 703.683.8100.

Library of Congress Catalog Card Number: 99-73474
ISBN: 1-56286-128-X

Table of Contents

Preface v

Section 1: The Role of Interactivity in Distance Learning 1

Chapter 1: Overview of Distance Learning Options for Trainers 3

Chapter 2: It's a Learner-Centered World! 11

Introduction to Chapter 3: On-Site Interaction and Distance
     Learning (What's the Difference?) 15

Chapter 3: Discovering the Difference Between On-Site and
     Distance Learning Interaction 17
Hank Payne

Introduction to Chapter 4: General Principles and
     Good Practices 41

Chapter 4: Distance Education Principles and Best Practices........43
Rosemary Lehman

**Section 2: Creating Interactivity Exercises for Learning
     Technologies** 61

Chapter 5: Framework for Making a Transition to Different
     Methods of Distribution...63

Chapter 6: Factors Influencing Media Selection 71

Introduction to Chapter 7: How to Move On-Site Exercises to
     Effective Interactive Distance Learning Exercises 79

Chapter 7: How to Adapt On-Site Exercises to Distance Learning
     Exercises: Practical Applications 81
Hank Payne, Lynn W. Payne, and Cissy Lennon

Section 3: Model Exercises in Distance Learning......................................**111**

Introduction to Chapters 8, 9, and 10: Case Studies and Lessons
Learned 113

Chapter 8: Creating Interactivity on the Web:
A DoD Case Study..115
Sharon G. Fisher and Will S. Peratino

Chapter 9: Addressing Engineering Curricula: An Audiographics
Case Study 127
Sue Faust

Chapter 10: Training for Interactivity: A Case Study of the
Wisconsin Public Service Commission 133
Bruce E. Dewey

Section 4: A Guide to Real-World Application **141**

Chapter 11: Bringing It All Together...143

Glossary of Distance Education Terminology 167

Resources..175

Dedication 189

About the Author 191

Preface

Why write this book, and more important, why write it now?

In my work with trainers and instructional designers, I hear them ask questions about the interactivity needed for effective and enjoyable distance learning courses. Sure, creating on-site interactive exercises is standard operating procedure for designing a course. Role plays, games, group discussions and exercises, reading, and the like have their own tried-and-true ways of being designed for learners located in the same room.

But, what about distance learning? If you have exercises that work well in your course, what do you do if you want to convert them to one or more distance learning distribution methods? Where does it say how to do it? My colleagues and I have looked hard at exploring different resources and have found excellent pieces of information. Yet, I felt that there needed to be a primer to increase awareness of what's different and to describe how to create interactive distance learning exercises that really work.

I wanted to ensure that you receive an excellent cross section of original writings by specialists in the field of distance learning instructional design. My colleagues who have contributed to this book are recognized experts and include Hank Payne, director of the Office of Training and Education, Occupational Safety and Health Administration; Cissy Lennon, the distance technology program manager for the Aircraft Certification Service at the Federal Aviation Administration; Rosemary Lehman, Bruce E. Dewey, and Sue Faust, all distance education and instructional design specialists who work at the University of Wisconsin-Extension; Lynn W. Payne, chief management strategist at Renaissance Strategies; Will S. Peratino, director of distance learning for the Defense Acquisition University; and Sharon G. Fisher, vice president of Human Technology. All sector specialists (public, private, and academic) whose work and experience are represented in this book are addressing the common threads of concern and priority that run through the effective interactive design of any course. Of course, each organization has its own individual and customized needs. You, the reader, can use this information as a foundation for building your own distance learning exercises that will really work for you.

Each section is designed to help illuminate the concept, pathway, and reasoning as to why we are emphasizing the importance of investing time and needed resources for interactive exercises. The sections are designed to support your own thinking processes as you convert your course content to different distance learning distribution methods. You can use the lists of key areas in the final chapter as a guide to help ensure that they are included in your total conversion process. You can use this guide as a primer or in conjunction with other sources and resources, or in both ways. For example, the 1997 ASTD book *Distance Learning: A Step-by-Step Guide for Trainers,* which I wrote with J. Richard Gividen, provides a broad foundation of information about distance learning. *Distance Learning Exercises that Really Work* is different in concept in that it focuses on one important aspect of distance learning—interactivity. It is not meant to be everything you ever wanted to know about distance-learning interactivity, but it is designed to provide a springboard for helping you think about your own distance learning exercises and create others.

As George Piskurich and Ethan Sanders (1998) state in their book *ASTD Models for Learning Technologies,* "The quality of the instructional design is much more important than the method in which it is delivered. The future of learning technologies, therefore, does not reside in how advanced the technologies become, but rather in how well we employ these technologies for learning purposes" (p. 45).

Alan Chute is the learning strategist of the Lucent Technologies Customer Care Institute and the Center for Excellence in Distance Learning. A statement he made stayed with me because of its importance. I don't recall where I read it, but I remember writing it down so that I would not forget it: "What we have found from distance learning research, however, is that learners need to interact. Adults need to be active participants in their learning, to share their life experiences."

Talking heads are out, interactivity is in. It's not a fad, it's reality for the successful trainer, instructional designer, and success of your distance learning initiatives.

With the learner in mind, I wish you great success as you help create a 21st-century learning environment to help your workforce excel. With a hybrid approach to providing education and training opportunities, your learners will help your organization effectively compete in a world judged by quality, timely, cost-effective, and precision-sharp application of information. The success of your distance learning initiatives will be measured by the remote site learners. Your creation of effective and enjoyable distance learning activities will help ensure your success.

I want to thank my professional colleagues who are dedicated to bringing the level of professionalism and validation to distance learning course delivery. Our distance learning community of qualified practitioners is small right now, compared with the overall numbers of qualified on-site training specialists. We are a tight-knit group and respond to each other's needs when, where, and however we can do so. I want to bring top distance learning specialists and their theories, applications, and years of experience to you, our reader. In this primer, we bring to you different perspectives based on actual results, not theory alone. I especially want to thank the contributors to this book: Hank Payne, Rosemary Lehman, Cissy Lennon, Lynn W. Payne, Sharon G. Fisher, Will S. Peratino, Sue Faust, and Bruce E. Dewey. As well, I want to thank them for reviewing the final manuscript and fine-tuning it to benefit our readers.

I want to thank my two editors at ASTD for their support and guidance during all phases of the book development. To Mark Morrow, I want to say thank you for pioneering this topic and being so patient. To Ruth Stadius, thank you for overseeing the copyediting process and for your creative recommendations. An author is part of an editorial team, and I appreciate the support from the entire ASTD team.

Karen Mantyla

Section 1:

The Role of Interactivity in Distance Learning

Chapter 1

Overview of Distance Learning Options for Trainers

INTRODUCTION

Did you ever feel backed into a corner because you had to get something done and felt you had no options? It's a smothering feeling when the road to your success appears closed, or really is closed, because of barriers beyond your control, such as time and money. It is a sinking feeling when you don't know which way to turn. Take classroom training as an example. You must train your workforce for all the mandated, functional, and soft skills required to achieve your workforce development goals. But time and money and perhaps inadequate staffing prevent you from having all the classes you need.

What about the learners? You post a course schedule, and some learners can't attend because of time constraints, others can't because of cost, and still others because of both time and cost. What's a trainer to do? Not get backed into a corner, for sure.

Distance learning offers you multiple and hybrid options for training your workforce. Forget the corner. It doesn't exist. You can color outside of the lines because there are none. Classroom training still exists, and most likely always will, but it no longer stands alone as the roadway to follow to achieve your goals.

WHAT IS DISTANCE LEARNING?

Many definitions of distance learning are available, but one that is pure and simple is, *Distance learning is learning without the physical presence of the instructor.*

Distance learning is learning without the physical presence of the instructor.

Normally, distance education is characterized by the following:

- Separation in place or time, or both, of one or more of the following: instructor and learner, learners from one another, and learners and learning resources.

- Interaction of one or more of the following: the learner and the instructor, learners and other learners, and learners and learning resources conducted through one or more media.

- Processes that employ a multiple set of delivery methods in the learning experience, such as written correspondence study, interactive audio, or video, computer, and other electronic technologies. Each of these may be used alone or in combinations. Use of electronic media is not necessarily required: Technology is a tool to aid the delivery and provision of educational opportunities.

- Processes may be in real-time interaction between learners and instructors, or asynchronous involving the access of instructors and materials by learners at any time.

Whether you choose that definition or another, you are sure to see the common thread of language focusing on the learner.

THE NEED FOR OPTIONS

The world around us mandates options. Needs don't fit into one category. The multifaceted training and education requirements fit into categories that include learners' needs, trainers' needs, and corporate needs.

Each category is complex, with driving forces based on individual agendas. Not a surprise, but it all adds up to intricate, interrelated goals and objectives.

Let's look at each, starting at the top of the distance learning pyramid.

LEARNERS' NEEDS

Learners need to have current information and real-world application training in order to effectively do their jobs. Just-in-time knowledge is no longer a frill, but a precision-sharp business strategy.

Workers may have jobs that have clearly defined skills. But what about filling in for someone else when needed? Or the increasing trend of cross-training to do several jobs? A learner is often put under a lot of pressure to perform, but often lacks the training to do it right. Learners need access to skill- and information-based training to perform well in any and all aspects of their jobs. They don't need the added pressure of being told to do a job without having proper information or training in how to do it, or both. Less-than-quality performance and costly mistakes are often a result of ineffective training. No one sets out to do a poor job, but people who've had less than effective training may have no choice. So, what's a learner to do?

Learners need guidance about education and training, and they need to be able to choose among a variety of training and educational options. And they need back-up support from the trainers on any and all questions they may have. Now, what about the trainers? How can they fulfill those learners' needs?

TRAINERS' NEEDS

Trainers' needs in the 21st century include having the time, resources, and knowledge about how to best facilitate the learning process for the learners. You might say, "This is not new!" And you'd be right. What is new is that information, change, and unprecedented demands are being made on the entire workforce. Doing more with less—we've heard it often. What are the best ways to do more with less? How can we, as trainers, ensure that we create a learning environment that is tailored to the needs of the 21st-century learner? The answer requires a shift in mindset away from the standard thinking of just on-site instruction.

There is no more job security as we knew it way back when. Job skills will be the new security for the 21st century, and solid and portable skills are and will become increasingly valuable. This recognition requires a shift in mindset away from the standard thinking.

As trainers, we have a very important role to play in creating the learning environment for the next century. If we want to continue our success as trainers, we need to ensure that we keep an open mind and continue our awareness of optional ways to support a quality learning organization.

Job skills will be the new security for the 21st century.

The training function is no longer a support function, but a critical operation for achieving the strategic goals of the organization. Leaders need to know that, and trainers need to ensure that their needs are met. Yes, I know, easier said than done. But any organization that does not recognize this new world of training and education will find it hard to survive in the new century. The trainers' needs include the following:

- awareness, knowledge, and training in using learning technologies to meet the training requirements of their workforce
- commitment from senior leadership in offering a hybrid approach to meeting strategic training needs
- funding support to acquire and maintain both hardware and software to keep up with the changing and new technologies
- coordinated and systematic working relationships with the information systems working arm of their organization
- ongoing education and training for technical, instructional systems design and for delivery of their distance learning lessons or courses, or both.

CORPORATE NEEDS

Even though the private, government, and academic sectors are different from one another in important ways, common threads of concern run through most organizations. Governmental organizations never talk about making a profit, but they must be as cost-effective as possible. Profit in nonprofit sectors may be described as earned reserves. However you say it, we all need to think of our business in the traditional business sense.

Corporate needs include:

- increased profit margins
- competitive advantages
- increased market share.

WHAT ARE YOUR OPTIONS?

The options at a trainer's disposal are many, based on the target audience size and profile, key learning objectives, and requirements for proficiency in any given area of learning. Even if you, the trainer, don't have internal learning technology systems already in place, the opportunities for joint-venture partnering are out there for the public, private, and academic sectors.

In *ASTD Models for Learning Technologies* (Piskurich and Sanders, 1998), the various types of options are laid out as a smorgasbord of choices from which to pick. We have been in need of a clear model with which to understand and select the best methods for our distance learning projects. This menu of options includes instructional methods, presentation methods, and distribution methods. Here are your options in the design, development, and delivery of your training and education modules and courses:

- Instructional Methods
    - case study
    - demonstration
    - expert panels
    - games

- group discussion
- lecture
- practical exercise
- programmed instruction
- reading
- role play
- simulation

- Presentation Methods

  - audio
  - CBT
  - electronic text
  - EPSS
  - groupware
  - interactive TV
  - multimedia
  - online help
  - teleconferencing
  - 3D modeling/virtual reality
  - video

- Distribution Methods

  - audiotape
  - cable TV
  - CD-ROM
  - computer disk
  - digital video disk (DVD)
  - electronic mail
  - extranet
  - Internet
  - intranet
  - LAN/WAN
  - satellite TV
  - tactile gear/simulator
  - telephone

— videotape

— voice mail

— World Wide Web (Piskurich and Sanders, 1998, p. 8)

Options? You bet! You are not boxed into a corner with only one way to teach. There are no corners.

The optional instructional, presentation, and distribution methods allow you to choose among vehicles and highways to best deliver your courseware. You can use one all by itself or, as the current trend stands, combine two or more for an interesting and enjoyable hybrid approach to learning.

SUMMARY

There are options for trainers and opportunities for learners everywhere! Suddenly learners can find a wealth of learning opportunities that are distributed by a variety of methods. More and more learners are looking to support their training and education needs and requirements on the basis of their just-in-time schedules.

REFERENCE

Piskurich, George, M., and Ethan S. Sanders. (1998). *ASTD Models for Learning Technologies: Roles, Competencies, and Outputs.* Alexandria, VA: American Society for Training & Development.

Chapter 2

It's a Learner-Centered World!

In times of change, learners inherit the earth, while the learned find themselves equipped to deal with a world that no longer exists. (Eric Hoffer)

INTRODUCTION

One of the major mindset shifts in the world of training and education is simple to state but somewhat difficult for many trainers to embrace. Simply stated, it's a learner-centered world. Why does it seem so hard to embrace that concept?

Formerly, many of us thought that trainers were the center of the learning universe. After all, we had to teach. Therefore, what we, the trainers, wanted to do and how we wanted to do it often drove the pathway of course development and delivery. In the picture of the 21st-century learner, we find that he or she will have a much more active role in how we select and design our just-in-time learning opportunities. Many learning options are available today, and they will most likely multiply by factors yet unknown in the next few year. Technologies bring the learning to the learner, and we, as trainers, must help facilitate the learning process, not try to control it or put our own emotional agendas first.

Comparable analogies include the one that the learners—your workforce—are your customers. Without customers, there is no business. We can easily identify with that from a purely business-minded thinking. Yet, without our workforce, we have no business. And, without a skilled workforce, our organizational business will have a tough time getting and keeping the customers who buy our product or services.

LEARNER SATISFACTION

When we design evaluation or assessment tools for distance learning, we should always include a section for learners to complete about their satisfaction with the course.

If we stay with the proven mindset that learners at the remote site measure the success of distance learning, our learner-centered evaluation methods will include designing tools that address these questions. In *Distance Learning: A Step-by-Step Guide for Trainers,* the authors suggest that trainers address learners' satisfaction in their assessment tools by covering the following:

How satisfied was the learner in the following:

- achieving learning objectives
- enjoying the learning experience
- knowing how to apply the subject content to work and to personal applications
- feeling comfortable asking questions
- getting answers to those questions
- being comfortable in the learning environment
- understanding how to use the technology
- participating in an active learning experience

- being able to use supporting materials in an easy-to-use, self-directed format
- getting support from the site facilitator. (Mantyla and Gividen, 1997, p. 134)

An additional question to ask is, How satisfied was the learner with getting help before, during, and after the distance learning event or course?

Success is measured at the remote site by the learners. As we each create our distance learning programs and 21st-century environment, it is helpful to keep that statement in mind. It seems like a simple statement, but it adds a new flavor to evaluations and assessments. (For these purposes, success equals measurable performance assessment and the enjoyment of the learning experience.)

There is so much at stake as you establish your distance learning programs and initiatives (corporate eyes will be watching). With each step you take of your design, development, and delivery efforts and deliverables, you will want to keep in mind that the learners measure success at the remote site.

Success is measured at the remote site by the learners.

As trainers, we are also learners who want opportunities to enrich our own learning base of knowledge. If we could get in the minds of the learners we train—and verbalize our own needs as learners—we might say we'd like the following:

- information on how to apply the learning concepts to my job
- ways to effectively keep up with changes
- to be proficient in my job tasks and responsibilities
- time to learn
- support in the learning process
- a motivational learning environment.

A lot to ask? Not really. As individual learners ourselves, we often become even more critical of the learning opportunities presented to us. Learners, in a universal sense, are the same way.

SUMMARY

The goal we want to achieve for our learners is to continuously improve the quality of the learning process. With on-site experience, we often know when and how to tweak the learning content and learning environment to improve the learning experience. With distance learning being relatively new to most learners (and trainers), the experience may often seem not as natural as traditional learning.

The goal we want to achieve for our learners is to continuously improve the quality of the learning process.

Learner-centered training and its surrounding environment is a new way of doing business for the training community. As time progresses, it will achieve the comfort level of on-site classes for both the learner and the trainer.

As long as we focus on helping to facilitate the learning process, we as trainers will know that the active learning experience will support learners' achievement, performance, and satisfaction. When that happens, we will have done our job.

REFERENCES

Mantyla, Karen, and J. Richard Gividen. (1997). *Distance Learning: A Step-by-Step Guide for Trainers.* Alexandria, VA: American Society for Training & Development.

Hoffer, Eric. http://www.masie.com. "Learning quotation," January 11, 1999.

Introduction to Chapter 3

On-Site Interaction and Distance Learning (What's the Difference?)

INTRODUCTION

The concept of interaction, or interactivity, in distance learning makes many trainers uneasy. On-site training experiences allow us to control when and how learners interact. We can choose to stop and start any of the instructional methods on the basis of what we see and hear, but we do not have the ability to see and hear every student in our classroom without walls. Through interaction in distance learning, however, we can improve the quality of the learning experience and ensure that we include as many learners as possible in an active learning experience.

KEY DIFFERENCES

So, what are the key differences between on-site interaction and distance learning? From the learners' perspective, the differences (both real and perceived) include:

- not being in the same physical location as the trainer
- not having the opportunity to network with peers for collaboration
- having to use technology often to complete the learning interaction process

- often being unsure about how to interact
- not being sure what the trainer expects
- not knowing how to ask questions (or appearing stupid in front of many people)
- being unsure about how to clarify learning content.

Many of the trainer's concerns are the same. Additional ones include:

- having training peers see or hear their instructional delivery, or both (When we are training on-site, we close the door and the learners are all ours.)
- not knowing how to use the appropriate technologies for interaction
- not wanting to look inexperienced using the technologies and associated hardware and software
- knowing how to foster interaction when you are separated from the learner
- how to facilitate interaction when trying to effectively use the learning technologies
- how to control many students at different locations.

The major concern both students and trainers have with distance learning that they don't have with on-site interaction is that they are not sure about what to do and how to do it. The key variables include using the technology, feeling confident about what will happen, and having the learning event or course be an enjoyable and useful experience.

One of the key training professionals in distance learning is Hank Payne. He has vast experience in the operation of a distance learning network and works closely with both instructional designers and trainers. He has written many articles and publications and is the president of the Federal Government Distance Learning Association. The following chapter is original writing just for this book, and you, our reader.

Chapter 3

Discovering the Difference Between On-Site and Distance Learning Interaction

Hank Payne

Director, Office of Training and Education
Occupational Safety and Health Administration,
U.S. Department of Labor

INTRODUCTION

Educators and trainers alike generally accept interaction as a critical component of good training and education. However, with the development of technologies that increase opportunities for interaction in modern classrooms and with the use of distance learning delivery systems, interaction may be one of the most misunderstood aspects of training and education.

The purpose of this chapter is to describe interaction as it relates to learning, to distinguish on-site interaction from interaction in distance learning environments, and to recommend techniques for increasing interaction in distance learning environments.

WHAT IS INTERACTION?

Interaction means different things to different people. For the following groups, interaction involves:

- *classroom instructors and trainers:* verbal questions and answers as well as discussions between learners and the instructor or trainer
- *computer-based multimedia instructional developers:* learners' responses to stimuli on the screen
- *two-way audio and video teleconferencing instructors:* verbal exchanges between learners and the instructor as well as exchanges among learners at different locations
- *two-way audio and one-way video teletraining instructors:* verbal exchanges between learners and the instructor and the verbal exchanges between learners at different locations; data responses from learners to questions from the instructor using student-response technologies.

Table 3.1 summarizes these different views.

Table 3.1. Instructors' and trainers' different views of interaction.

	Spoken and Written Q and A Discussions	Response to Stimuli on Screen	Exchanges at Different Locations	Data Responses
Classroom instructors and trainers	X			
Computer-based multimedia instructional developers		X		
Two-way audio instructors	X		X	X
Video teleconferencing instructors	X		X	
One-way audio instructors	X		X	X

THE CONCEPT OF INTERACTION

Interaction is a requirement in most learning models and instructional theories (see, for example, Bloom, 1976; Gagne, 1985; Kruh and Murphy, 1990; Merrill, 1983; Reigeluth, 1983; Wager and Mory, 1993). Interaction is a requirement for maximum effectiveness to occur in such instructional events as the following (Bates, 1990; Smith and Ragan, 1992):

- gaining attention
- stimulating attention
- maintaining attention
- informing learners of the instructional purpose
- presenting information
- asking and answering questions
- providing feedback on performance.

Virtually all adult learning models acknowledge some level of interaction as a requirement for learning as well (see, for example, Knowles, 1980; Knox, 1986; Long, 1983; Wlodkowski, 1985). Additionally, learners interact with other learners in sharing their misery about the course and in mutual learning (Egan, Ferraris, Jones, and Sebastian, 1993; Thiagarajan, 1978). It is apparent that some form and level of interaction are required for the learning process.

Virtually all adult learning models acknowledge some level of interaction as a requirement for learning.

A WORKING DEFINITION OF INTERACTION

An acceptable working definition of *interaction* is dependent upon your instructional situation. That is, one's definition of interaction depends on the delivery method being used. Popular delivery methods today include the following:

- resident classroom instruction
- one-way video and two-way audio teletraining

- two-way audio and video teleconferencing
- audioconferencing
- multimedia CD-ROM instruction
- Internet and intranet instruction.

The capabilities of the technology used with a delivery method determine the parameters for interaction of that delivery method.

As an example, with most one-way video and two-way audio tele-training delivery systems, it's possible for learners to have verbal exchanges with the instructor or trainer, who is at a different location, as well as with other learners, who are also at different locations. Technology with greater capabilities extends the limits of the interaction. With newer interactive response systems for use with one-way video and two-way audio teletraining delivery systems, it's also possible to have data responses from the learners back to the instructor. That is, in addition to verbal interaction, the instructor or trainer is able to pose true-false, yes-no, multiple choice, and numeric value questions to the learners, who answer the questions using the keypad functions of the response system. These systems provide all learners with the opportunity to answer all questions. These systems also record learners' response data and allow the responses to be rolled up by question and displayed back to the learners as a check on their learning.

Interaction is "the degree to which an individual actively participates in an information exchange."

For the purposes of this chapter, *interaction* is defined as "the degree to which an individual actively participates in an information-exchange" (Portway and Lane, 1994, p. 305). However, the term means different things in different distance learning environments, as this discussion will show.

TYPES OF INTERACTION

The instructional process uses four types of interaction: learner-content, learner-instructor, learner-to-learner, and learner-interface

(Moore, 1989; Hillman, Willis, and Gunawardena, 1994), as table 3.2 shows.

The first type of interaction is learner-content interaction (Moore, 1989). This type of interaction involves the conversation each learner has with himself or herself about the information and ideas contained

Type	Description	Purpose or Effect
Table 3.2. Types of interaction in the instructional process.		
Learner-content interaction	Conversation learners have with themselves about the information and ideas contained in the instruction.	This interaction is to find some relationship with existing information that will allow learners to remember the new information.
Learner-instructor (or trainer) interaction	Interaction between the instructor or trainer and learners about the information and ideas presented in the instruction.	Instructors and trainers consider this interaction very desirable, and learners consider it essential.
Learner-to-learner interaction	Interaction learners have with other learners about the ideas and information in the instruction.	Learners complain if this interaction is missing.
Learner-interface interaction	Learner interacts with the technology in order to interact with the content, the instructor or trainer, and other learners.	If interaction takes too much effort, there may be less available for learning and other interactions.

in the instruction (Oliver and McLoughlin, 1996; Moore and Kearsley, 1996). The purpose of this type of interaction is for learners to find some relationship with existing information that will allow them to remember the new information. Educators consider this interaction of learners with the content the "defining characteristic" of education (Moore and Kearsley, 1996).

The second type of interaction is learner-instructor or trainer interaction (Moore, 1989). This is interaction the instructor or trainer has with learners about the information and ideas presented in the instruction (Moore and Kearsley, 1996). Instructors and trainers consider this type of interaction very desirable for the learning process, and learners regard it as essential for the learning process (Bates, 1990; Moore and Kearsley, 1996; Oliver and McLoughlin, 1996; Ritchie, 1991).

Learner-to-learner interaction is the third type of interaction (Moore, 1989). This is the interaction learners have with one another about the ideas and information presented in the instruction (Bates, 1990; Moore and Kearsley, 1996; Oliver and McLoughlin, 1996). When this type of interaction is missing, learners often complain about the lack of interaction in instruction.

The fourth type of interaction is learner-interface interaction (Hillman, Willis, and Gunawardena, 1994). In this type of interaction, learners must interact with the technology in order to interact with the content, the instructor or trainer, and other learners (Hillman, Willis, and Gunawardena, 1994). Many trainers and educators are concerned that if the requirements for interacting with the technology take a great deal of mental effort, less mental effort will be available for learning and interacting with the content, instructor, and other learners. As a result, less learning may take place.

SYNCHRONOUS AND ASYNCHRONOUS INTERACTION

When most people think of interaction, they think of real-time interaction in which people are all involved at the same time. This kind of interaction that involves an instructor or trainer with learners and learners with one another basically at the same time occurs in the following:

Same time interaction is called synchronous interaction.

- traditional resident classrooms
- teletraining
- video teleconferencing environments.

When a student interacts with the computer for a multimedia CD-ROM lesson, the interaction is taking place in real time, that is, as the student works at the computer. Same time interaction is called *synchronous* interaction (Moore and Kearsley, 1996).

Interaction may also take place at different times. In a correspondence course, for example, a student mails a question to the instructor or trainer, and the instructor or trainer mails back a response. Interaction may also occur at different times in a course that a student takes over the Internet. A student emails a question to a chat room and has to wait until the next day to get responses from classmates. Interaction that occurs at different times is called *asynchronous* interaction (Moore and Kearsley, 1996).

WHY IS INTERACTION IMPORTANT?

Interaction is important to the learning process for a number reasons. Although instructors and trainers and learners have different perspectives on why interaction is important, they also agree on some of the reasons.

Interaction that occurs at different times is called asynchronous interaction.

INSTRUCTORS' AND TRAINERS' PERSPECTIVE

The reasons instructors and trainers consider interaction important can be grouped into the following general areas:

- conducting instruction
- evaluating learners' achievement of objectives
- evaluating adequacy of the instruction and instructional content
- evaluating personal traits of individual learners.

Conducting Instruction

Interaction of an instructor or trainer with the learners enhances a number of events that occur during instruction, including the following:

- gaining, stimulating, and maintaining the learners' attention
- informing learners of the instructional purpose
- presenting information
- asking and answering questions
- providing feedback on the learners' performances. (Bates, 1990; Smith and Ragan, 1992)

Some of the interactive techniques are to help instructors or trainers grab and keep the learners' attention. At the same time, some of them give them information on how well they are delivering the instruction and learners are receiving it. Following are some of the techniques instructors and trainers use:

- posing thought-provoking questions
- making controversial statements and asking learners to respond
- asking questions that require learners to apply information
- reviewing learners' performance on a written exam or a hands-on performance exam.

Evaluating Learners' Achievement of Objectives

Instructors and trainers use both formal and informal checks to evaluate how well participants are learning the information and achieving the objectives. Formal checks include graded or critiqued written and performance examinations and assessments. Instructors or trainers give part of the feedback; managers, supervisors, and peers may also comment. Employees who learn how to pave a street or sell a new product would likely get on-the-job critiques, whereas those who learn a new tax law would probably get a written examination. Informal checks include pop quizzes and questions instructors or trainers ask participants during class discussions.

If all the learners are not achieving the objectives, interaction can help instructors or trainers evaluate the adequacy of the instruction and instructional content.

If all learners are achieving the objectives, the instructors or trainers can feel secure that both the instructional delivery and the instructional content are sound for the learning objectives. If all the learners are not achieving the objectives, interaction can help instructors or trainers evaluate the adequacy of the instruction and instructional content.

Evaluating Adequacy of the Instruction and Instructional Content

When evaluating how well learners have achieved the learning objectives, instructors and trainers often find that despite their best efforts, a number of learners did not achieve certain learning objectives. When this happens, good instructors and trainers want to analyze the instruction and the content to identify and correct any problems. Analyzing the instruction requires the instructor or trainer to interact with the learners about the delivery of the material. The instructors or trainers should ask the learners the following:

- what worked for them in the instruction
- what helped them obtain the instruction
- what did not work for them in the instruction
- what interfered with their obtaining the instruction
- what was confusing.

An analysis of the instructional content requires instructors and trainers to analyze test items to determine those areas or instructional objectives that learners did not master. They should validate any areas or instructional objectives that learners did not master. During the interaction with learners, instructors or trainers should seek to determine the reason learners didn't achieve the objectives. There are a host of potential causes for them to consider, such as the following:

- a lack of prerequisite instruction
- a need to review prerequisite instruction
- a lack of examples

- poor use of poor examples
- misunderstood or undefined terminology.

Interaction is clearly necessary for evaluating the adequacy of the instruction and instructional content.

Evaluating Personal Traits of Individual Learners

Lastly, instructors and trainers should observe learners' interactions with one another to evaluate such personal traits as:

- leadership ability
- ability to follow other learners' leadership
- ability to follow instructions
- ability to work with others
- ability to work alone.

During the interaction with learners, instructors or trainers should seek to determine the reason learners didn't achieve the objectives.

Instructors or trainers should provide learners with feedback about their strengths and their weaknesses, and recommend how they can improve the traits that need work.

LEARNERS' PERSPECTIVES

Learners' perceptions of why interaction is important can be grouped into the following general areas:

- receiving the instruction
- evaluating performance and achievement of learning outcomes and objectives
- evaluating instruction
- evaluating individual personal traits
- misery sharing and mutual learning.

Receiving Instruction

Instructors' and trainers' interactions with learners and learners' interactions with one another during the delivery of the instruction help learners determine the degree to which they are receiving the instruction. The questions and answers that the instructors or trainers and the learners give one another assist learners in determining if they understand the information and ideas. Additionally, the learners' discussions and exchanges with one another help them confirm for themselves their understanding of the information and ideas. Learners do not have to be personally involved in these interactions for them to confirm their learning. That is, they do not have to personally ask or answer questions or engage in verbal interactions with the instructor or trainer or other learners. Many times, learners who do not personally interact will have their unasked questions answered through the interactions initiated by other learners, thus confirming their learning.

Evaluating Their Performance and Achievement of Learning Outcomes and Objectives

Learners use various types of interaction to evaluate their own performance and how well they've mastered the learning objectives. The interactions they use are as follows:

- results of both formal and informal evaluations and examinations
- interaction with instructors or trainers.

Interaction also helps them measure how well they are doing in comparison with other learners. When learners answer questions on examinations or pop quizzes, they want to know if they answered correctly and how well they did in comparison with their classmates. Without this interaction, learners may become anxious and frustrated because they don't know if they are learning, and that frustration could interfere with their ability to focus on learning.

Evaluating Instruction

Many courses provide learners with the opportunity to interact with the instructor through an end-of-course evaluation. These evaluations often give learners the opportunity to grade the instructors or trainers, the course delivery, and the course content. This is the learners' opportunity to provide feedback to the instructor or trainer on what worked and what didn't work. This is also the learners' opportunity to comment on the relevancy of the course content. In short, it is the learners' chance to help improve the course.

Evaluating Individual Personal Traits

Learners use a variety of instructional events to evaluate themselves on how well they perform as a leader and a follower and on how well they do the following:

- work with other learners to achieve assigned tasks
- follow directions
- work without direct supervision through exercises assigned and evaluated by instructors or trainers.

Keep in mind that learners will often want to confirm their evaluations with feedback from instructors or trainers and frequently from other learners.

Misery Sharing and Mutual Learning

Lastly, learners interact with other learners both in sharing their misery about the course and in mutual learning (Egan, Ferraris, Jones, and Sebastian, 1993; Thiagarajan, 1978). Learners share with other learners their feelings of fear and frustration related to the course. They may feel afraid, for example, that they won't master the subject, or they may feel frustrated by an assignment they've been struggling with. By sharing their pain, learners realize that they are alike and are struggling equally with the course. Learners also interact with other learners outside of class in mutual learning, or confirming their learn-

Learners interact with other learners both in sharing their misery about the course and in mutual learning.

ing with that of others in their group. This type of interaction takes place more frequently than many instructors or trainers acknowledge.

INTERACTION IN RESIDENT CLASSROOMS AND AT A DISTANCE

Interaction that occurs in resident classrooms is different from interaction that occurs in distance learning courses, although they have many aspects in common. Instructors and trainers need to recognize the differences and select instructional techniques that make the best use of interaction at a distance.

INSTRUCTORS' AND TRAINERS' PERSPECTIVE

Instructors' and trainers' perspectives of distance learning can be grouped into the following areas:

- conducting instruction
- evaluating learners' achievement
- evaluating instructional content
- evaluating learners' personal traits.

Conducting Instruction

One of the more noticeable ways in which interaction in resident classrooms differs from interaction in distance learning environments is in the delivery of instruction. Many distance learning delivery technologies do not allow the instructor or trainer to see the learners. These types of distance learning technologies include:

- one-way video
- one-way audio teletraining systems
- audio systems
- CD-ROM technologies
- asynchronous Internet and intranet technologies.

With these technologies, nonverbal communication is lost. Instructors and trainers can't read learners' body language and facial expressions.

Instructors and trainers need to compensate for the loss of non-verbal communication by building in opportunities for learners to interact with them at other sites. The purpose of these interactions is for the instructors and trainers to receive feedback from the learners on how well the instruction is being received. With two-way video distance learning technologies, it is still a good idea to build in interaction opportunities to check how well the learners are receiving the instruction. The resolution of many two-way video technologies is not of a sufficiently high quality to allow instructors and trainers to effectively receive and correctly interpret nonverbal communication from the learners.

Instructors and trainers need to compensate for the loss of nonverbal communication by building in opportunities for learners to interact with them at other sites.

Evaluating Learners' Achievement

Instructors and trainers will not be able to personally proctor learners' examinations and evaluations, as they are accustomed to doing in resident classrooms. To compensate for that, instructors and trainers should take a variety of steps to ensure the test is fair and learners get proper feedback. Following are some helpful steps:

- Instructors and trainers must use on-site proctors to ensure that the integrity of the examination or evaluation process is not compromised.
- They need to communicate any special instructions for administration of the examination or evaluation to the proctors, including instructions on what to do with the complete examinations and evaluations.
- Instructors and trainers should provide learners with a review of the examination as soon as possible so they can verify how well they did in achieving the learning objectives. This step is to compensate for the usual delay in getting graded examinations back to learners in most distance learning environments.

It takes longer than in resident classrooms because proctors usually have to mail exams to the instructor, and the instructors have to send them back to the proctors to distribute to the learners at each site.

- Instructors and trainers should go over the examination again after learners have received their graded examinations to clarify any areas where learners may still be unclear.

Evaluating Instructional Content

In resident classrooms, learners complete end-of-survey questionnaires to help instructors determine the adequacy of the instruction and the content. Learners in distance learning courses can complete the same questionnaires, but because they will be administered at remote sites, proctors should pass them out and collect them. Again, instructors or trainers will need to communicate with the proctors before administration of the surveys to convey any special instructions and directions for what to do with the complete surveys. If the distance learning technology provides the capability for a discussion with the learners, instructors may also want to hold one for an evaluation of the course.

Evaluating Learners' Personal Traits

One-way video distance learning technologies don't have the capabilities to permit instructors or trainers to observe the interaction between learners, which is necessary for evaluation of such personal traits as leadership, ability to follow others, and ability to work with others in a group. Instructors and trainers can get peer feedback by conducting group feedback sessions after the exercises, although it is difficult for them to do that because they can only communicate with one group at a time. If proctors are available, they can provide the instructor with feedback. To get effective feedback, instructors and trainers should provide proctors with a standardized protocol for evaluating each learner and with directions in using it.

Even if the distance learning technology provides for two-way audio and video, it is still a difficult challenge for the instructor or trainer to effectively view group interactions at all sites. The instructor or trainer may want to observe one or two groups in detail, but get feedback from proctors at all sites. The instructor may want to talk about these traits in general with the entire class, leaving individual feedback to the proctors at each site.

The very nature of distance learning environments changes how instructors and trainers interact with learners. In general, in distance learning courses, instructors:

- will have less verbal interaction with learners
- will need to design opportunities for interaction into their courses at strategic locations
- will have to rely on the assistance of proctors and team leaders for feedback on learners' behavior at each site.

Instructors and trainers can deliver instruction just as effectively at a distance as they do in resident classrooms.

Despite these challenges, instructors and trainers can deliver instruction just as effectively at a distance as they do in resident classrooms.

LEARNERS' PERSPECTIVE
Receiving Instruction

In distance learning environments in which instructors and trainers can't see learners, many of the learners don't pay as close attention to the instruction as they would in resident classrooms. This lapse can cause them anxiety when examination time approaches. Learners need different types of stimuli to ensure they pay attention and participate in the course. The purpose of these interactions is for the learners to verify how well they are receiving the instruction. Two-way video distance learning technologies don't present the same challenges as the one-way technology, but instructors will still have to work hard to keep learners engaged. Because the instructor or trainer isn't present or readily accessible, learners assume more of the responsibility for learning in distance learning environments than they do in resident classrooms.

Evaluating Achievement of Learning Outcomes and Objectives

The taking of examinations and evaluations, both formal and informal, is different in resident training environments than in distance learning environments because the instructor isn't in the room during the examination. A proctor should be present to ensure the integrity of the examination process. The proctor does the following:

- passes out the examination
- reads and explains directions for taking the examination
- answers any questions learners may have about the examination
- collects the examinations as learners complete them.

The proctor won't have the correct answers for the examination and will mail them to the instructor or trainer for grading. As a result, learners may have to wait longer for the results than they would for courses they take in resident classrooms. Learners should ask for a review of the examination as soon as possible. This will help them confirm how well they are achieving the learning objectives and will help lower any anxiety they feel about their performance.

Evaluating Instruction and Content

Learners also interact with the instructor to evaluate the instruction, which is usually done at the end of the course or section. The same surveys used in resident classrooms can be used in distance learning environments. A proctor will administer the survey, as he or she administered examinations. One possible advantage here is that because the instructor or trainer will not be in the room with learners in distance learning environments, learners may be more candid with their evaluations of the instruction.

Evaluating Individual Personal Traits

Learners will be able to evaluate their individual personal traits during instructional events in distance learning environments, just as they did in resident classrooms. For those distance learning delivery systems that are capable of facilitating group work, learners can evaluate themselves in the following ways:

- as leaders
- as followers
- how well they performed in working with other learners on activities
- how well they follow directions
- how well they can work without the direct oversight of the instructor.

Some organizations will provide proctors for remote receive sites, and some will not. For those distance learning environments that provide proctors, there will be no perceptible change for the learners. For those that do not, learners may find it difficult to get group work completed correctly and on time, and will find it difficult and uncomfortable to ask the instructor for assistance.

Misery Sharing and Mutual Learning

Lastly, learners in resident classrooms interact with other learners by sharing their misery and learning together. These interactions are somewhat difficult to do in distance learning environments. Distance learning courses that use one-way or two-way video delivery technologies usually have small groups of learners at each site. These small groups can provide some outlet for learners in misery sharing and mutual learning. Learners can ask the instructor or trainer for a few minutes at the start of class for learners to interact with each other about the course. Unfortunately, CD-ROM delivery systems, being primarily self-paced, do not provide an opportunity for this kind of interaction. Chat rooms set up as part of courses delivered by Internet or intranet can help learners with their misery sharing and mutual learning. Keep in mind that the asynchronous nature of the Internet and intranet may frustrate learners who need to share their feelings with other learners or need to verify their learning.

SUMMARY

Probably the biggest difference for learners in distance learning environments is that they have a greater responsibility for their learning than they normally have in resident classrooms. Learners in distance learning environments will perceive they work harder than they do in resident classrooms, and depending on the technology, learning strategies, and other variables, they may. Despite these differences, learners in distance learning environments can expect to learn as much as they do in resident classrooms, if not more.

This chapter has defined the concept of interaction. It showed that the definition of *interaction* is situation and technology dependent in distance learning environments. The chapter identified four types of interaction and provided an understanding of the synchronous and asynchronous nature of interaction. It discussed the more common perceptions of interaction from the perspective of instructors and trainers and from learners' perspective, as reviewed in table 3.3.

Learners in distance learning environments can expect to learn as much as they do in resident classrooms, if not more.

In the final section, the chapter described how interaction in distance learning environments differs from interaction in resident classrooms, and it recommended ways to maximize interaction in distance learning environments. Interaction is the key ingredient to successful distance learning courses. It must be used effectively for both instructors and trainers and learners to achieve learning objectives and to be satisfied with the distance learning experience.

Table 3.3. Perspectives on importance of interaction.

	Conducting or Receiving Instruction	Evaluating Learners' Achievements or Achievement of Outcomes and Objectives	Evaluating Instruction and Content	Evaluating Learners' Personal Traits	Misery Sharing and Mutual Learning
Instructors or trainers	Provides information on effectiveness of delivery	Tells how well students are learning the information and meeting objectives	Tells how well the instruction is designed to help learners achieve the objectives and outcomes	Provides the instructor with information on learners' selected personal traits	
Learners	Determines degree to which perceive they're receiving information	Tells how well they've achieved objectives and how they're doing compared with others	Tells the instructor how learners felt about the instruction and the course content	Provides learners with information on how well they work alone or with others in groups	Allows learners to confirm their learning and to share with other learners how they are feeling about the course

THE AUTHOR

Hank Payne is director of the Office of Training and Education, Occupational Safety and Health Administration (OSHA), U.S. Department of Labor. He is responsible for training federal and state compliance officers, state consultants, employers, and workers on the recognition, identification, and abatement of hazardous and unsafe conditions in the workplace. He is responsible for the conduct of OSHA courses by the OSHA Training Institute (OTI), administration of the Susan Harwood Training Grant Program, and the development of outreach material. Payne also oversees the OTI Education Centers, which offer OSHA-developed courses primarily for other federal agency employees, employers, and workers.

Payne worked for the Federal Aviation Administration (FAA) from 1991 to 1998, where he served as manager of its distance learning program. He was directly responsible for the FAA's Interactive Video Teletraining Program, a satellite-delivered technical training program. He was also directly responsible for the design of an innovative approach to studio design, which reduced the number of people required for a satellite broadcast from eight to 12 down to one.

Payne is past president of the Federal Government Distance Learning Association, a chapter of the U.S. Distance Learning Association. He is on the board of directors of the U.S. Distance Learning Association and is president of the Government Alliance for Training and Education.

REFERENCES

Bates, A.W. (1990). *Interactivity as a Criterion for Media Selection in Distance Education*. Paper presented at the meeting of the Asian Association of Open Universities, Jakarta, Indonesia. (ERIC Document Reproduction Service No. ED 329 245)

Bloom, B.S. (1976). *Human Characteristics and School Learning*. New York: McGraw-Hill.

Egan, M.W., C. Ferraris, D.E. Jones, and J. Sebastian. (1993). "The Telecourse Experience: A Student Perspective." *ED Journal, 7*(5), J-1–J-8.

Gagne, R.M. (1985). *The Conditions of Learning* (4th ed.). New York: Holt, Rinehart, and Winston.

Hillman, D.C.A., D.J. Willis, and C.N. Gunawardena. (1994). "Learner-Interface Interaction in Distance Education: An Extension of Contemporary Models and Strategies for Practitioners." *The American Journal of Distance Education, 8*(2), 30–42.

Knowles, M.S. (1980). *The Modern Practice of Adult Education: From Pedagogy to Andragogy.* New York: Cambridge.

Knox, A.B. (1986). *Helping Adults Learn.* San Francisco: Jossey-Bass.

Kruh, J.J., and K.L. Murphy. (1990, October). *Interaction in Teleconferencing: The Key to Quality Instruction.* Paper presented at the Twelfth Annual Rural and Small Schools Conference, Manhattan, KS.

Long, H.B. (1983). *Adult Learning: Research and Practice.* New York: Cambridge.

Merrill, M.D. (1983). "Component Display Theory." In *Instructional Design Theories and Models,* (pp. 163–185), C.M. Reigeluth, editor. Hillsdale, NJ: Lawrence Erlbaum.

Moore, M.G. (1989). "Three Types of Interaction." *The American Journal of Distance Education, 3*(2), 1–6.

Moore, M.G., and G. Kearsley. (1996). *Distance Education: A Systems View.* New York: Wadsworth.

Oliver, R., and C. McLoughlin. (1996). *An Investigation of the Nature and Form of Interactions in Live Interactive Television.* Proceedings of Ed Tech '96 Biennial; Conference of the Australian Society for Educational Technology, 115–122.

Portway, P.S., and C.E. Lane. (1994). *Guide to Teleconferencing and Distance Learning* (2d ed.). San Ramon, CA: Applied Business teleCommunications.

Reigeluth, C.M. (1983). *Instructional Design Theories in Action.* Hillsdale, NJ: Lawrence Erlbaum.

Ritchie, H. (1991). *Interactive, Televised Instruction: What Is Its Potential for Interaction?* Proceedings of the Second American Symposium on Research in Distance Education (pp. 55–58). University Park, PA: American Center for the Study of Distance Education.

Smith, P.L., and T.J. Ragan. (1992). *Instructional Design.* New York: Macmillan.

Thiagarajan, S. (1978). "The Loneliness of the Long-Distance Learner." *Audiovisual Instruction, 23*(1), 22 and 39.

Wager, W., and E.H. Mory. (1993). "The Role of Questions in Learning." In *Interactive Instruction and Feedback,* (pp. 47–69), J.V. Dempsey and G.C. Sales editors. Englewood Cliffs, NJ: Educational Technology Publications.

Wlodkowski, R.J. (1985). *Enhancing Adult Motivation to Learn.* San Francisco: Jossey-Bass.

Introduction to Chapter 4

General Principles and Good Practices

INTRODUCTION

When you hear the terms *general principles* and *good practices,* you're liable to respond with the commonsense question, "What makes them good?"

As trainers, we often look to benchmarking from other organizations that have a track mark of excellence in the activity that interests us. Distance learning is no exception. There have been many benchmarking reports of those people and organizations that have either received awards or have validated the effectiveness of their distance learning programs.

I once did a benchmarking report for a client and had a hard time coming up with five organizations that excelled in their distance learning programs. Now, the list has expanded to give everyone a look into the public, private, and government sectors and the organizations that have become the benchmark for their area. No reinventing the wheel is necessary for a good foundation.

As technology and the domino-effect applications change, more people will serve as the pioneers of application.

GOOD PRACTICES

Thomas L. Russell's book *The No Significant Difference Phenomenon,* published by North Carolina State University in 1999, is of value to everyone who wants to know good practices and wants to ensure that research validates the effectiveness of distance learning.

In seeking out one of the benchmarking bests in distance learning, I turned to the University of Wisconsin-Extension at Madison. It is a benchmarking organization for all sectors and is recognized as one of the leaders in distance learning. Rosemary Lehman shares her experience to highlight the general principles and good practices that the University of Wisconsin uses in its distance learning programs. She uses the term *distance education,* which is often substituted for *distance learning.* Whichever term you use, here are her experiences and a validated foundation for you to build upon. Once you read them, you are likely to perceive them as intuitively sensible.

Chapter 4

Distance Education Principles and Best Practices

Rosemary Lehman

Senior Outreach and Distance Education Specialist
Instructional Communications Systems
University of Wisconsin-Extension

INTRODUCTION

My colleagues and I at Instructional Communications Systems, have learned through our work in distance education that instructors are involved not merely with designing a course, a program, or a session but also with designing an overall experience for the learners.

This concept is continually reinforced as we work with instructors at colleges and universities, with government groups, nonprofit organizations, and business and industry. One example that illustrates this concept is a videoconference session we held with a number of instructors, some of whom were in the process of teaching their first semester via compressed video (a form of two-way video, two-way audio that is delivered via dial-up digital phone lines or fiber networks), and some of whom were preparing to teach their first courses in a few months. During this session the more seasoned instructors shared their experiences with those new to this technology.

In telling their stories, the seasoned instructors talked about their course content and how it was designed to take advantage of the potential of the technology, but many other factors entered into and dominated their presentations and dialogue. Following are some of their comments:

- *French instructor:* "I often have the feeling, because this is a new experience and people want to see what it's like, that I'm an amoeba on a slide under a microscope. . . . As for the teaching experience, I want to focus on the support staff, on the enormous role that they play in every session. Without them, this just wouldn't happen!"

- *Education instructor:* "I know what you mean, about the amoeba under the microscope. At times I feel like I'm in a fishbowl. I had a group of nine visitors drop by, unannounced. . . . What I'm experiencing with the class is that there is this distance that separates you from the learners, so you have to find ways to reach across that distance. And it's important to incorporate variety into the session, through the use of various appropriate media and to reach out to learners at the remote sites, to question them frequently, to engage them and keep them involved so they're less likely to tune out."

- *Writing instructor:* "Now I need to tell you what I feel like— there's a pack of dogs nipping at my heels and that sometimes they get very close. I had release time for planning, but I needed more, at least this first time—I see you're all nodding in agreement. . . . As for the class, with the learners, as I teach, communication is essential. I've encouraged a number of ways to communicate, for example, fax, email, and regular mail, and of course, phone. This is very important, to keep in touch and to keep the communication flowing."

- *Education instructor:* "Many learners don't know how to learn via distance education. They have to be trained and oriented. I was surprised to find out how many learners were unfamiliar with email and the process of creating and receiving attachments. From now on I won't make assumptions about learners' technology skills."

- *French instructor:* "Time is really involved in teaching this way. I've spent a tremendous amount of time developing class materials. My syllabus alone is 30 pages long. It helps bring organization to the experience. Learners know exactly what will be covered each day. This detail is very useful if something happens on the system."
- *Writing instructor:* "I've found, too, that organization and clarity are critical, that I need to be very specific in my instructions. And when I do the final evaluation, I'll need to include areas like the technology, the sites, the support. This is a different and more complex situation we're in."

MORE THAN MEETS THE EYE

These instructors make clear that teaching via technology involves more than designing content for learning. The role of teaching is changing. First, there is the additional pressure and risk placed on the instructor who is venturing into the new territory. Then that instructor must address the many needs of the learners he or she may never meet in a face-to-face situation. The instructor must do the following:

More is involved in teaching via technology than designing content for learning.

- reach out to the learners
- make certain that they have had the same type of orientation that the instructors have had
- ensure they're comfortable in this new learning environment
- see to it that they have the skills to use the required resources
- create a variety of appropriate formats and strategies that actively engage and involve them so they are less likely to tune out
- keep the communication flowing
- create a presence and a virtual room
- know who they are

- team with others in the design, management, and support processes
- evaluate the processes in a more expanded way by, for example, adding evaluation of the instructor, the environment, the equipment, the site coordinator, and the overall experience
- take into consideration the many variables in this more complex and new kind of interactive experience.

PREPARING INSTRUCTORS FOR THE NEW INTERACTIVE EXPERIENCE

Three guiding principles can help trainers as they prepare their programs for instructors who are embarking on teaching in a distance education environment. These principles provide guidance regardless of the subjects the instructors will teach and how much they know about distance education.

PRINCIPLE NUMBER ONE: REACH THEM WITH THEIR LOVE TO INSTRUCT

It is challenging to work with instructors in this new environment and prepare them for teaching via interactive technology. Instructors come with varying levels of enthusiasm, knowledge of technologies, and experience with practical application. Regardless of their differences, instructors have one thing in common: They love to instruct. This is where we try to reach them—with their passion for teaching and working with learners. We assure them that this will still be their focus, but that they will now have an expanded set of tools at their disposal.

Regardless of their differences, instructors have one thing in common. They love to instruct.

PRINCIPLE NUMBER TWO: PROVIDE A MEANS FOR VOICING ISSUES AND CONCERNS

In the ideal world, the instructors' institutions or organizations would have developed and carried out a needs assessment and actively involved the instructors in the following:

- creating a strategic plan
- selecting the appropriate technologies to meet specific needs
- developing policy that places value on instructing via technology.

This is the world we need to work to-ward, one in which thoughtful and effective planning both involves and supports instructors. In many instances in the real world, instructors come into the training situation filled with issues and concerns that need some degree of resolution. We take this into consideration and provide time for discussion. It's also very reassuring for instructors to hear that others have the same concerns.

PRINCIPLE NUMBER THREE: INSTRUCTING VIA THE TECHNOLOGY MEANS EXPERIENCING THE EXPERIENCE

Instructing via technology means "experiencing the experience." Often our design team is asked to train instructors or trainers about videoconferencing, in a face-to-face situation. We do everything we can to discourage this type of training because it is impossible to just talk about something that centers on the physical experience of doing. Instructing via technology is an intellectual, physical, social, and mul-titasking situation, with new variables that need to be experienced. Talking about them just doesn't do. It would be like teaching some-one how to play the piano or play golf by hearing about it, rather than by actually learning the skills, practicing, and playing.

TRAINING INSTRUCTORS FOR THE NEW INTERACTIVE EXPERIENCE

The principles that we use in working with instructors in the distance education interactive environment are grounded in the following seven key areas:

- understanding the learner
- knowing the environment
- being a team player
- developing formats and strategies

- creating interaction activities, visuals, and print materials
- integrating support
- monitoring for quality.

It is essential to take these areas into consideration during the distance education development and design process. An in-depth description of these areas appears in *The Essential Videoconferencing Guide: 7 Keys to Success* (Lehman, 1995).

PRINCIPLES IN KEY AREA ONE, UNDERSTANDING THE LEARNER

Research and our training experiences tell us that instructing via technology is most fruitful when a learner-centered approach is used. This approach places learners at the center of the educational experience, focuses on their diverse needs, and places value on the expectations and experiences they bring to the learning situation. The first step in this type of approach is to get to know the learners. This is relatively easy to do in the traditional classroom where you are face-to-face. It's more difficult when learners are at a distance. In this instance, instructors need to create ways to compensate for the loss of personal contact. Following are some ways instructors can overcome the distance and get to know the learners:

- *Survey questionnaire:* This document is designed to obtain information that faculty members need for learner-centered course development, such as previous videoconferencing experience, previous education, personal interests, course expectations, and special needs. It is sent out well ahead of the first session.
- *Phone calls:* This is another option for obtaining information from learners. While phone calls are more personal, they are also more time-consuming for the instructor than the survey questionnaire.
- *Biography, or bio forms:* A third option, the bio form, includes the same request for information as the survey questionnaire and the phone calls.

The purpose of each is to find out about previous experience, education, interests, special needs, and course expectations, so that instructors can design an optimum learning experience.

Different environments lend themselves to different methods of personalizing. Following are the recommended methods for some environments:

- videoconferencing course
  — large name tags
  — site seating charts

- multisite situations
  — site identification signs

- audiographics sessions (that is, the simultaneous transmission of voice and computer graphics over ordinary phone lines that also allows for annotation, writing, and drawing on the screen)
  — site charts

- computer courses
  — email
  — chat room tools
  — telephone.

Whenever possible, instructors should call learners by name and check off their names on their seating chart as they respond, making certain that everyone has an equal chance for involvement.

PRINCIPLES IN KEY AREA NUMBER TWO, KNOWING THE ENVIRONMENT

Instructors must become comfortable with the technology, media, and software. Three activities that are essential to help them feel comfortable are

- knowing the components of the new environment
- discovering the differences between the traditional classroom and the new interactive environment
- practicing with the new tools.

Trainers should assist instructors in gaining this understanding by doing the following:

- having them actively experience the environment
- introducing them to the many options they have
- letting them practice.

More and more, a distance education course will emphasize one technology, but it will integrate with and blend in with other technologies and media. Teaching via all types of technology incorporates intellectual, physical, and social skills. All of these skills need to be accommodated through training, giving the instructors a certain level of comfort.

PRINCIPLES IN KEY AREA NUMBER THREE, BEING A TEAM PLAYER

Instructors are often surprised to find out that they need to depend on a team of people to develop their sessions and have them run smoothly. Being a team member and working with a team is not always easy for instructors who have been a one-person show. But as instructors experience this new environment, they are grateful for the additional expertise and support. Remember our French instructor's statement about the importance of the support staff: "Without them, this just wouldn't happen." Team makeup varies and is dependent on the following:

Instructors are often surprised to find out that they need to depend on a team of people to develop their sessions and have them run smoothly.

- the type of technology
- the complexity of the course
- the budget
- the available personnel.

PRINCIPLES IN KEY AREA NUMBER FOUR, DEVELOPING FORMATS AND STRATEGIES

At the very core of training for this new interactive experience is the development of the appropriate formats and strategies that work best for the specific learning situation. When using the learner-centered approach, it is critical to have learners gain a thorough understanding of the content area first and then to have them construct knowledge in a way that is meaningful to them. This process encourages "deep learning" (Gibson, 1998a).

To develop formats and strategies that will accomplish this, instructors need to do the following:

- look at their overall content
- decide on scope and sequence
- decide on outcomes and how the outcomes will be evaluated
- modularize the content into sessions
- modularize each session into short sequences for variety and appropriate use of media interface or software, or both
- think interactively and visually
- develop contingency plans just in case Murphy's Law—whatever can go bad will go bad—goes into effect during the session.

Interaction and involvement are key to thoroughly understanding a subject and to deep learning (Gibson, 1998a). Instructors can obtain the desired interaction and involve learners by doing a number of things, such as:

- creating a well-structured knowledge base that will form the foundation for interaction
- providing a context that will motivate the learners
- integrating appropriate interaction activities
- designing the interaction to take place with others, the materials, and the technology and media.

Instructors have the knowledge base and in most cases have already done an excellent job of structuring that base for the traditional classroom. Now, having worked through the formats and strategies for this new experience, they must make a concentrated effort to consider carefully the technology and media they are using and to decide on how they can best motivate the learners, engage them, and encourage them to interact and construct knowledge that will be meaningful to them.

Interaction can take place within a number of areas:

- Moore's learner-teacher interaction, learner-learner-interaction, and learner-contact interaction (1989)
- learner-medium interaction (Hillman, Willis, and Gunawarndna, 1994)
- Gibson's learner-context interaction (1998b).

The types of interaction, and variations on them, are limited to the instructor's imagination. We've identified five separate categories with the interactivity spectrum in figure 4.1 and a way to formulate a healthy balance of activities with our interactivity guide pyramid in figure 4.2. The types of activities an instructor selects will depend on the course content and the technology and media used.

How can you suggest a healthy menu for interactivity? Colleague Mavis Monson suggests the following as an integral part of the interactivity guide pyramid:

Figure 4.1. Interactivity Spectrum.

Interactivity Spectrum (from simple to complex)				
Present	**Personalize**	**Show**	**Participate**	**Question**
mini lecture	name use	objects	readings	Q&A
expert guest(s)	postcards	pictures	fax/email	black box
interviews	bio form	trigger video	groupwork	debates
case study	bio booklet	participation video	field trips	quizzes
storytelling	dialogue	simulation	lab sessions	fish bowl

Interactivity Spectrum developed by Rosemary Lehman, UW-Extension, 1995, *The Essential Videoconferencing Guide: 7 Keys to Success.* Instructional Communications Systems, UW-Extension: Madison, WI. Reprinted with permission from Instructional Communications Systems.

Figure 4.2. Interactivity Guide Pyramid.

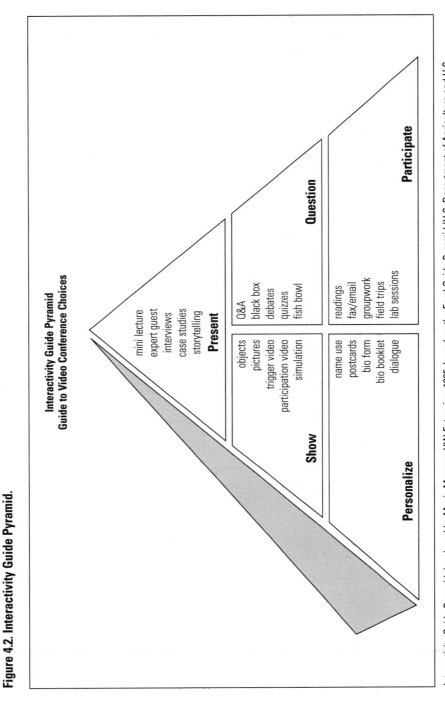

**Interactivity Guide Pyramid
Guide to Video Conference Choices**

Present

mini lecture
expert guest
interviews
case studies
storytelling

Show

objects
pictures
trigger video
participation video
simulation

Question

Q&A
black box
debates
quizzes
fish bowl

Personalize

name use
postcards
bio form
bio booklet
dialogue

Participate

readings
fax/email
groupwork
field trips
lab sessions

Interactivity Guide Pyramid developed by Mavis Monson, UW-Extension, 1995, based on the Food Guide Pyramid (U.S. Department of Agriculture and U.S. Department of Health and Human Services, 1993). Reprinted with permission from Instructional Communications Systems.

Choose:

3-5 servings of activities from the **Personalize Group**

3-4 servings of activities from the **Participate Group**

2-3 servings of activities from the **Show Group**

3-5 servings of activities from the **Question Group**

sparingly   from the **Presentation Group** **(if one-way presentation)** and use more generously if mixed with activities from the other groups

PRINCIPLES IN KEY AREA NUMBER FIVE, CREATING INTERACTION ACTIVITIES, VISUALS, PRINT MATERIALS

Thinking visually in course preparation means thinking about what your learners are seeing at all times during the course. It also means developing appropriate, meaningful, and well-designed visuals. Visuals are often a part of the interaction process and can be specifically designed to be an interaction activity (Cyrs, n.d.). Print materials are an important component to all distance education courses and are an integral part of all distance learning. Print is another important tool (not to be considered lightly, even though not in an electronic format) that serves as a component in all distance education courses.

PRINCIPLES IN KEY AREA NUMBER SIX, INTEGRATING SUPPORT

Support in distance education takes many forms:

- instructor support
- learner support
- site support
- resources support
- special needs support.

Support for an instructor begins with full support from that individual's organization through:

- active involvement in technology and software selection
- a voice in the process of policy development
- adequate release time and value placed on the field of distance education
- team support for the courses delivered via distance learning.

Support for the learner comes through:

- a one-call-for-all number that learners can access for answers to any questions about the course or learning experience
- a help number for technology assistance
- a thorough orientation to distance education and the various technologies the learners might use
- an understanding of course protocol
- easy access to resources
- prompt instructor feedback and instructor access.

Other types of necessary support include the following:

- *Site support:* Both technical and site coordinator support are necessary to make the course happen.
- *Resources support:* Distance education with its geographically dispersed sites and learners requires special support to work with libraries and media personnel for the arrangements that need to be made for easy and equal resource access.
- *Special needs support:* It's important to ensure that equal access is available.

PRINCIPLES IN KEY AREA NUMBER SEVEN, MONITORING FOR QUALITY

During the past few years, there has been an increased interest in evaluation and the development of methods of evaluation that include continuous feedback sheets, projects, practical experience, portfolios, and group evaluation, along with the standard essay and multiple choice exams or as components of them. Evaluation is the process of monitoring for quality, and quality is what we're after in all learning experiences. The evaluation of interactive distance education experiences is important not only to evaluate learner outcomes, but also to evaluate the effectiveness of the distance education experience and its long-term impact. This type of evaluation is in its infancy. What we do know is that if appropriate technology is used and courses are well designed, they are as effective as traditional classroom courses, if not more effective than them.

FOLLOWING THE PRINCIPLES FOR BEST PRACTICES

As instructors become more and more comfortable with creating interactive experiences in distance education, they are refining their skills and creating effective practices that, for these early days of distance education, can certainly be called best practices. As instructors share their stories with peers who are embarking on the distance education experience, their understanding of this new process continues to grow. We're confident that the instructors you heard from earlier in this chapter are on their way to developing best practices. They are enthusiastic instructors committed to working with the technology and to learning to use it effectively. They have a good understanding of the principles, have planned well, and practiced both alone and with multipoint critiqued rehearsals. They also have strong institutional support, a new chief information officer, excellent site support staff at all of their 13 sites, a listserv for communicating with each other, a growing list of resources on their new Website, the support of technical and instructional design personnel, and a growing network of peers to share information with.

While these instructors are in the beginning stages of developing and implementing their courses, there are a growing number of best practices in the University of Wisconsin system that have already proven themselves and are being emulated by other universities and institutions. Following are four examples: resort planning, technical Japanese, collaborative nursing program, and Lotus LearningSpace:

- *Resort Planning:* Resort Planning is a point-to-point video-conferencing course taught by Bill Ryan, a lecturer at UW-Madison. Ryan integrates videoconferencing, computer graphics, print materials, fax, and email into his sessions. Via audio or video, he brings into each classroom guest expert resort owners from across the country. Ryan has his learners form teams at each site to simulate resort team planning. Each student on a team has a specific role to play, such as budget or marketing. Through this process the learners problem solve real-life situations and prepare for the real world. Ryan likes being able to see his learners as well as talk to them, and he likes the capability to bring in guests in a variety of ways. It is a highly interactive experience. His course evaluations show that his remote learners are learning equally as well as those in a traditional classroom and that his remote learners consider the course a positive experience. This is an exemplary course that fills the practical needs of many learners who would not be able to take the course if it were not offered via distance education.

- *Technical Japanese:* Now in its seventh year, Technical Japanese is a technical language course that Professor Jim Davis of UW-Madison teaches via audiographics. With audiographics, he can watch learners write technical terms, critique their work through a shared document, and talk to them as well. Davis likes the flexibility of the medium, its ease of use, and its low cost. Audiographics is a relatively low-cost technology because it operates over regular phone lines. In addition, it is computer-based, so both faculty and learners find it easy to use. Extensive examination score analysis of both remote and campus sites shows that there is no statistical difference between the two groups. This course meets a specific need for engineers and has been able to reach an increased number of learners nationwide through this interactive technology.

- *Collaborative Nursing Program:* This series of multipoint courses is the result of the collaborative efforts of four UW nursing schools and one UW Nursing Department. The series of courses in the Collaborative Nursing Program uses a variety of technologies: the World Wide Web, online courses, audiographics, videoconferencing, and audioconferencing as well as fax and email. Interaction is central to the design. A coordinating group comprised of representatives from each nursing institution has helped to work out the interinstitutional barriers of credit, cost, course content, and technology selection. This highly successful series of courses is the answer to a need that surfaced through statewide surveys. It provides an accessible way for Wisconsin nurses to earn their baccalaureate degree. Because of its success, the University of Wisconsin is now considering offering the course nationally.

- *Lotus LearningSpace:* Lotus LearningSpace is authorware that the University of Wisconsin Learning Innovations is using with a number of UW faculty, who have found it a successful way to teach online. It is providing them with a consistent interface in which course materials are easily accessible. LearningSpace components that provide this interface are the Schedule (syllabus), MediaCenter (media library), CourseRoom (threaded discussions—that is, that separate a discussion into specific topics—and assignment area), and Profile and Assessment databases (class roster and quizzes). The security of the system provides a sense of privacy and trust for both faculty and learners, and the activity-based design (learners engage in legal analyses, debates, and case studies) and threaded discussions create extensive interaction. Discussion is carefully structured and is central to the course, not an ornament. LearningSpace is complex authorware with a steep learning curve. University of Wisconsin Learning Innovations is working successfully with instructors to design effective online courses that provide anywhere, anytime learning.

At Instructional Communications Systems, we have a unique opportunity to assist in the design and support of many of these courses and to watch them as they are developed and refined. Through these observations and experiences, we are convinced that effective courses start with the following:

- a strong instructional content base
- an instructor who is willing to venture into new areas
- an understanding of the technologies and media that are selected
- a commitment to follow underlying distance education design principles for designing distance education experiences
- the support of institutions to make this all happen.

SUMMARY

Good principles and good practices start with a solid layer of what would be important to us if we were the distance learning student. Starting with that in mind, common sense becomes the first layer in the foundation, followed by all aspects of being on the receiving end of a quality learning experience. As you prepare your distance learning environment, become familiar with the different technology options and then, based on your training needs assessment, determine which technology, or better yet, which hybrid mix would have the best application options.

Many of us have heard the expression, "Been there, done that." In distance learning, many have pioneered the way for all of us. The sound principles listed here are not theoretical in nature; they are based on hundreds of distance learning experiences. We sometimes get black and blue marks when we try something new. This chapter was presented to help you start off with a proven base of good practices.

You'll add your own good practices to this foundation, as every organization has unique needs. Now that the base is in place, we'll move on to the actual creation, or framework, for developing interactivity exercise models that can be used for different learning technologies.

THE AUTHOR

Rosemary Lehman, is senior outreach and distance education specialist at Instructional Communications Systems at the University of Wisconsin-Extension. She has 27 years of experience in media production, design elements, and training. She holds a B.A. in English from Lawrence University, an M.A. in television and communication arts, and a Ph.D. in distance education and adult learning, both from the University of Wisconsin-Madison. Lehman has consulted and trained for audio, television, satellite, and compressed video. She has developed and published training materials, coordinated symposia, and presented at distance education conferences. She has also taught at the University of Wisconsin-Extension for the past eight years.

REFERENCES

Cyrs, Tom. (n.d.). *Teleclass Teaching: A Resources Guide,* (2d edition). Las Cruces, NM: Center for Ed Development, New Mexico State University.

Gibson, Chere. (1998a). Guest speaker via audio during the presentation Beyond the Keypad at the International Teleconferencing Association EXPO98: Boston.

Gibson, Chere, editor. (1998b). *Distance Learners in Higher Education: Institutional Responses for Quality Outcomes.* Madison, WI: Atwood.

Hillman, D., D. Willis, and C. Gunawarndna. (1994). "Learner Interface Interaction in Distance Education: An Extension of Contemporary Models and Strategies for Practitioners." *The American Journal of Distance Education, 8*(2), 30–42.

Lehman, Rosemary. (1995). *The Essential Videoconferencing Guide: 7 Keys to Success.* Madison, WI: Instructional Communications Systems, University of Wisconsin-Extension.

Moore, Michael. (1989). "Editorial: Three Types of Interaction." In *The American Journal of Distance Education, 3*(2), 1–6.

Section 2:

Creating Interactivity Exercises for Learning Technologies

Chapter 5

Framework for Making a Transition to Different Methods of Distribution

INTRODUCTION

For trainers to make the transition to distance learning, they'll find it helpful to list the items, ideas, or concepts that form the basis of the interactive exercises that they now do on-site. This list will help them develop a framework for the transition. For example, with on-site learning, trainers identify tasks and objectives and on the basis of them, they create and select the appropriate interactivity. For distance learning, they will do the same thing. Then they will identify which distance learning technology best suits the task, objective, and experience. They shouldn't begin any of these steps, however, until they are sure they have the right mindset.

MINDSET

Before you can actively make the transition to distance learning, you should take a look at your mindset about distance learning. Do you really feel it can work? If not, don't proceed until your questions, concerns, and priorities are addressed. Right now, distance learning is not the norm in delivering training. On-site learning still is, and most trainers must overcome their own doubts before they can change from the tried-and-true to the new. But we must. We have to do it for the learners' sake and must realize that distance learning is here to stay because it can reach more people effectively and cost-efficiently. In fact, it will become the dominant way to deliver training in the 21st century.

ASTD and other organizations offer peer networks for trainers who have questions about the value of distance learning. You can also gain insights into the value of distance learning by reading case study examples and real-world situations and by speaking with many people who use distance learning—even elsewhere around the world. For example, I received an email from a professor in Munich who was "forced" to look at distance learning by his institution. He asked if there was any validated research on the effectiveness of satellite delivery. I pointed him to a book that has over 254 research reports that target just what he was looking for. The book, by Thomas L. Russell, is *The No Significant Difference Phenomenon,* published in 1999 by North Carolina State University.

My reason to position this important aspect first is that I have seen many trainers and their respective organizations move on without first addressing trainers' concerns. If you or your organization move forward without first addressing your concerns, your doubts and skepticism may overshadow even the most commonsense discussions. It is important to start your distance learning journey with a confident approach that is based on clarifying your questions or dealing with your concerns. Whatever questions you may have, other trainers have most assuredly asked as well. The answers might help you get ready to begin embracing the how-to-do-it phase in your professional development. For those of you who have already moved to the new learner-centered distance learning mindset, great going! Sometimes, it's not easy, but you will see that your dedicated efforts at

If you or your organization move forward without first addressing your concerns, your doubts and skepticism may overshadow even the most commonsense discussions.

each step will yield positive results for you, the learners, and your organization.

CURRENT INTERACTIVITY EXERCISES DESIGNED FOR ON-SITE DELIVERY

Take a look at each course activity by examining the steps in the instructional systems design model. If the activity makes sense and works well on site, then you should determine what method of distribution you may use for distance learning. Ask yourself what learners can and can't do using each method of technology you're considering.

You may need to create a hybrid approach for an exercise. The on-site exercises are done in front of the trainer. The learner completes them there, and the trainer sees, hears, and takes the next steps according to how the learners are progressing.

In the world of distance learning, the trainer is not "there." So, how can you make the transition to exercises that use different types of learning technologies? One of the first steps is to refer to the list of items, ideas, and concepts from the on-site activities, and decide which ones pertain as well to the distance learning activity. For each one, ask the following:

- Can learners complete it on their own?
- Do they need specific guidance as they go along?
- Do they need to see a picture or other visual or reference materials in order to complete the exercise?
- Do they need to collaborate with team members?
- How do they ask questions?
- Will there be any testing along the way or at the completion?
- How do they currently apply the learning exercise to their job?

The answers to these questions will help you decide how to make the transition from the on-site exercise to distance learning. For example, if you have an on-site team collaboration exercise in which groups of learners are put in teams, you might consider forming teams at each remote site for the team collaborative exercise. In this fashion, teams can work together prior to the live event and during the live event to discuss their findings.

You may want to create a combination of learner activities that include readings before the distance learning course or event and conclude with an exercise after. You can create the activities in print, audio or video support, Web based, or something else. Prework often helps trainers accomplish the learning objectives, and it forms an excellent base from which to springboard interactivity during a live event, such as satellite or online learning.

It is important for trainers to understand the various learning technologies. You don't have to be a techie, but you'll want to know which learning technologies are best suited for the applications you need for the learners' needs. Knowledge of the technology will give you a good foundation for making decisions about which distribution methods are best for which courses.

In the next chapter, we will look at the factors that will influence your media selection and help you pick the right learning technologies for your course delivery.

Trainers sometimes are pushed into using a technology because it's the favorite of a person in power, such as a company's president or director. Several clients have told me that they were mandated to deliver courses on the Web even though that technology didn't suit the learning content or the workforce didn't have the proper equipment to receive the training. Although it isn't always possible to forestall mistakes like these, trainers can try by doing the following: Become knowledgeable about distance learning. Make recommendations based on facts, not emotions. If indeed you are mandated to use something that might not be the right fit, you can look at your options for a hybrid approach that could satisfy the needs of the learner and the mandate.

As a start, consider the advantages and disadvantages of a variety of distance learning technologies. These lists appeared originally in *Distance Learning: A Step-by-Step Guide for Trainers,* by Karen Mantyla and J. Richard Gividen (1997):

- *Interactive television:* Learners see and hear the instructor by viewing live television. Instructor receives feedback and interacts with learners through an audio connection or a view response keypad, or a combination of both.

  — **Advantages**
  — Ability to transmit live video and audio to multiple sites in widely dispersed locations
  — Significant cost-efficiencies for large audiences
  — Large inventory of facilities already in place available for use
  — When used with viewer response pads, allows data input from learners.
  — **Disadvantages**
  — Requires extensive equipment to broadcast signal
  — Requires installation of satellite downlink dishes at remote sites
  — Requires thorough training on equipment at remote sites. (1997, p. 35)

- *Computer-based training:* Learners use personal computers and software. They range from simple, mostly text-based screens to more complex software that includes video, sound, and animation.

  — **Advantages**
  — Allows self-paced training
  — Inexpensive distribution costs
  — Evaluation built into instruction
  — Enables use of exiting videos and visuals.

— **Disadvantages**
— High costs for development
— Lengthy development timelines
— Individuals need moderate computer literacy to use. (1997, p. 44)

- *Internet- and intranet-based training:* Learners and instructors interact via a network of linked computers using email, online computer conferencing, and email message boards. Course and reference materials are made available online for learners to view or download.

— **Advantages**
— Materials readily updated
— Inexpensive distribution costs
— Access to multiple courses with training on single piece of Web software
— Self-paced training.
— **Disadvantages**
— Moderate to high degree of computer literacy to create Web training sites
— Video and sound transmission extremely limited
— Security measures to prevent unwanted viewing. (1997, p. 48)

- *Video teleconferencing:* Learners and instructors see and hear one another through two-way transmission of both video and audio.

— **Advantages**
— Allows the instructor to see the learners
— Flexibility of multiple "instructor" sites
— Enables learners to interact with each other visually.
— **Disadvantages**
— High costs for transmission of courses
— High costs for establishing sites
— Difficulty of managing visual interaction with several sites. (1997, p. 39)

- *Audioteletraining:* Learners and the instructor can hear one another through a conference-call with the instructor via speakerphone or convener. Usually the instructor distributes learner materials before the teletraining.

  — **Advantages**
  — Very inexpensive
  — Easy to set up
  — Minimal training on equipment
  — Uses existing phone lines.
  — **Disadvantages**
  — Not appropriate for training requiring live interactive video
  — Requires distribution of visual materials before the event.
  (1997, p. 23)

- *Audiographics:* A conference-call audio interaction coupled with the ability for learners and the instructor to share computer-generated graphics and slides with one another.

  — **Advantages**
  — Very inexpensive
  — Easy to set up
  — Minimal training on equipment
  — Uses existing phone lines
  — Provides ability to share charts, graphs, digitized photos
  — Whiteboard capability.
  — **Disadvantages**
  — Not appropriate for training requiring live interactive video
  — May require distribution of computer-image files before the event
  — Requires some degree of computer literacy to create course materials. (1997, p. 25)

SUMMARY

The first steps in the transition to different methods of distribution include identifying the learners' needs by examining the tasks and objectives, targeting the courses that will be adapted, and identi-fying the applications that you need. You will help increase the odds for success in creating your interactivity exercises by becoming knowl-edgeable about the different types of technologies available and then finding the best match for your learning experience.

REFERENCE

Mantyla, Karen, and J. Richard Gividen. (1997). *Distance Learning: A Step-by-Step Guide for Trainers.* Alexandria, VA: ASTD.

Chapter 6

Factors Influencing Media Selection

The selection of instructional media and tools should reflect their accessibility to learners. A distance education program should incorporate a technology base that is appropriate for the widest range of students within that program's target audience. (DEOS News, 1998)

INTRODUCTION

There have been many efforts at helping trainers choose the best instructional media for teaching people specific jobs. The result is that there are numerous books and articles about media selection. Whichever one you choose, it is most important that you choose a method (that is, a logical tool) that will become part of your decision-making process as you make the transition from on-site to distance learning course materials.

In using a selection tool, it is vital to ensure that you clearly identify your course tasks, objectives, and requirements, including the learners' and trainers' needs. The technology should become seamless in the delivery of the course and not obstruct the learning process.

Various federal government organizations, such as the Federal Aviation Administration, the Internal Revenue Service, the Environmental Protection Agency, and the Defense Logistics Agency, have created these logical tools. You don't need to reinvent the wheel here, as validated wheels are already in use and have traveled many miles!

Figure 6.1 shows the media selection instrument developed by the DLA Center for Training, Education, and Development (DCTED) of the Defense Logistics Agency. It gives the key result areas to consider for each course that you may want to convert. It is important that you rank the importance of each area in your evaluation and decision-making process.

The instrument lists training situations in rows by number. The lettered columns correspond to different media or combinations of media. To use the tool, highlight the rows that apply to your training situation. For example, if your learners have varied levels of experience in the subject or course, you'd highlight row 37 and the corresponding columns. Interactive courseware, Internet training, on-the job training, and a reference manual are all media that would best serve the needs of these learners. You would total the checks in each column for the rows you select and then determine which training method best suits your learners.

One important concept to remember is, One size fits all does not fit anymore.

Many trainers are using more than one method of distribution to effectively teach their course by distance learning. This diversity is predicated on the fact that:

One important concept to remember is, One size fits all does not fit anymore.

- Learning objectives and tasks don't lend themselves to just one area.
- Budgets may not allow for use of a certain delivery system.
- Learners may not have access to equipment for one or more of the selected methods.

Figure 6.1. A logical tool for selecting media.

MEDIA SELECTION INSTRUMENT
Developed by the DLA Center for Training, Education, and Development (DCTED)

Instructions: Highlight each row that applies to your training situation. Next total the number of checks highlighted in each column and write the total at the end. Then determine which media or combination of media would best train personnel. A separate analysis must be completed for a cost comparison.

A. Interactive Courseware
B. Interactive Video Teletraining
C. Instructor-Led Internet Training
D. Classroom Instruction
E. Videotape
F. Audio Tape
G. Audio Graphics
H. Computer Conferencing
I. OJT
J. Paper-Based Self-Study
K. Job Aid
L. Reference Manual
M. Train-the-Trainer

	A	B	C	D	E	F	G	H	I	J	K	L	M
1. Audio skills are required		✓	✓	✓	✓	✓	✓	✓	✓				✓
2. Consequence of error on the job is severe	✓	✓	✓	✓	✓	✓	✓	✓	✓	✓	✓	✓	✓
3. Small equipment is used				✓				✓	✓				✓
4. Large equipment is used								✓	✓				
5. Hazardous situations must be demonstrated					✓								
6. Instant recall of information is required	✓	✓	✓	✓		✓	✓	✓	✓	✓	✓	✓	✓
7. Job aids are psychologically unacceptable	✓	✓	✓	✓	✓	✓	✓	✓	✓	✓	✓	✓	✓
8. Job area too dangerous or disruptive	✓	✓	✓	✓	✓	✓	✓	✓	✓	✓	✓	✓	✓
9. Physical movements need to be demonstrated		✓		✓	✓				✓	✓	✓	✓	✓

(continued on page 74)

Figure 6.1. A logical tool for selecting media (continued).

	A	B	C	D	E	F	G	H	I	J	K	L	M
10. Physical movements need to be performed by the students		✓		✓									✓
11. Provide rapid non-linear access to information	✓		✓						✓		✓	✓	
12. Standardization of training is required	✓		✓		✓	✓				✓	✓	✓	
13. Subject matter changes more often than every six months		✓	✓	✓			✓	✓	✓				
14. Synthesis, problem solving, creativity required		✓		✓			✓		✓				✓
15. Task is done on computer	✓			✓			✓	✓	✓		✓	✓	✓
16. Task is done very seldom	✓		✓		✓	✓			✓		✓	✓	
17. Task is simple (done in less than 5 minutes)	✓		✓						✓		✓		
18. Task is very complex		✓		✓			✓	✓	✓		✓	✓	✓
19. Task sequence is critical											✓		
20. Task varies often		✓		✓			✓	✓	✓				
21. There are many details seldom used	✓											✓	
22. There are too many details to remember	✓		✓									✓	
23. Students must be able to interact with other students		✓	✓	✓			✓	✓	✓				✓
24. Students will need to be sold on the concepts or procedures prior to instruction				✓	✓	✓							
25. Task involves personal interface		✓		✓									✓
26. Real-time interaction between students and instructor required		✓	✓	✓		✓	✓	✓	✓				✓

Factor												
27. Content can be taught only at one geographic location		✓		✓		✓	✓		✓			✓
28. Lack of available instructors	✓	✓		✓	✓		✓	✓	✓	✓	✓	✓
29. Lack of student travel time	✓	✓	✓	✓	✓		✓	✓	✓	✓	✓	✓
30. Privacy of student inquiry is important			✓					✓				
31. Student load will be sporadic	✓	✓	✓	✓	✓		✓	✓	✓	✓	✓	✓
32. Student schedules are inflexible	✓	✓	✓	✓	✓		✓	✓		✓	✓	✓
33. Curriculum changes will have short notice		✓	✓	✓	✓		✓		✓			
34. Training must be just-in-time	✓	✓	✓	✓	✓		✓	✓	✓	✓	✓	✓
35. Short time-frame to complete all training	✓	✓	✓	✓	✓		✓	✓	✓	✓	✓	✓
36. Short time-frame to complete course development			✓			✓			✓		✓	✓
37. Students are at extremely varied levels of competence	✓	✓		✓				✓	✓		✓	
38. Employees have low reading level		✓	✓	✓	✓		✓	✓	✓			✓
39. Training is knowledge oriented	✓		✓	✓	✓		✓			✓	✓	
40. Training is skill oriented		✓	✓	✓				✓	✓			✓
41. Supervisors are not experts	✓	✓	✓	✓	✓		✓	✓	✓	✓	✓	✓
42. Valid performance tests are possible only on the job												
43. A major portion of the information can be found on the Internet			✓					✓				
TOTAL HITS												
TOTAL MISSES												

Source: Developed by the DLA Center for Training, Education, and Development (DCTED) of the Defense Logistics Agency.

(continued on page 76)

Figure 6.1. A logical tool for selecting media (continued).

Description of methods of instruction.

A. Interactive Courseware—Electronically programmed training which includes a variety of media (e.g., written narrative, graphics, video, sound), provides instruction, checks for understanding and feedback, and allows for some branching and student selection of activities.

B. Interactive Video Teletraining—Instructor-led instruction delivered over a video-satellite system or terrestrial line based video broadcast system.

C. Instructor-Led Internet Training—Training provided over the Internet directed by an instructor. May include such functions as chat rooms, bulletin boards, Internet page reading assignments, Internet research assignments, etc.

D. Classroom Instruction—Instruction at a specific time and place to a group of students and led by instructor.

E. Videotape—Instruction videotaped and distributed on tape or CD-ROM.

F. Audio Tape—Instruction audio-taped and distributed on audio tape.

G. Audio Graphics—Instructor-led instruction delivered over lines to students through computer systems. In this method students can hear the instructor's voice and see on computer the same thing displayed on the instructor's computer.

H. Computer Conferencing—This instruction is similar to video teleconferencing except that each student is sitting at a computer which has a camera attached. The students see and hear the broadcast (instructor or other student) on their computer.

I. On-the-Job Training—Training which takes place while a student is performing the job.

J. Paper-Based Self-Study—This method includes any type of written self-study or home study materials. No instructor is required for the student to complete the training.

K. Job Aid—A brief list of the steps to complete a job. May also include other essential job information. A job aid should be designed in a format and placed in a location so as to be readily useable while performing the job.

L. Reference Manual—A written document containing all detailed information required to perform a job. The document should be designed to make information quickly accessible for all required job tasks.

M. Train-the-Trainer—Functional experts are trained to deliver training part time in lieu of using full-time professional trainers.

It is a common-sense approach to ensure that the profile audience has access to the technologies you select.

The factors that influence media selection should be based on clearly defined facts rather than emotion. For example, many trainers feel that they can't effectively teach unless they can see their students. This reaction is surely normal, but does it stem from a training requirement? Is it critical that students see the trainer in order to learn?

If you are not familiar with one or more of the media in the DLA chart, you would do well to take a course or attend a workshop or other program in which you could see these various methods in operation. In chapter 5, you read about the pros, cons, and applications, but by seeing the methods in action, you can assess how they work, just as a learner might. Many colleges, universities, and training companies deliver their courses through a variety of media, so you can choose to take a course on site, via satellite, or on the Internet, for example. You can query the listserv DEOS-L@LISTS.PSU.EDU to find out where to find course listings by media type.

The factors that influence media selection should be based on clearly defined facts rather than emotion.

SUMMARY

Trainers use an instructional systems design approach to make sound decisions in the design and the development of a course. To achieve their learning objectives for distance learning, trainers should, therefore, take a systems approach to selecting the right media or combination of media for our distance learning course delivery.

REFERENCES

DEOS News. (December 16, 1998). The Distance Education Online Symposium, volume 8, number 12.

Media Selection Instrument, developed by the DLA Center for Training, Education, and Development (DCTED), Defense Logistics Agency, Columbus, Ohio 1998.

Introduction to Chapter 7

How to Move On-Site Exercises to Effective Interactive Distance Learning Exercises

Trainers often ask, "I have an on-site exercise. How do I adapt it to a distance learning format?" What if I want to use a computer-based technology? What if I use satellite delivery? What are the differences that I need to think about as it relates to the exercises and interactivity?

In chapter 7, you will get the perspectives of three distance education specialists, Hank Payne, Lynn W. Payne, and Cissy Lennon. On the basis of their experience and education, they will provide you with different model exercises and tips to use as you make the transition to different distribution methods. They will give you different types of scenarios so you'll have a cross-sectional look at what to consider as you adapt your program and have outside vendors do work for you.

These authors have a reputation for both reality and excellence in distance learning. Theory is great, but application is the dominant driver of why we are writing this book for you. Here are their thoughts and recommendations.

Chapter 7

How to Adapt On-Site Exercises to Distance Learning Exercises: Practical Applications

Hank Payne

Director, Office of Training and Education
Occupational Safety and Health Administration,
U.S. Department of Labor

Lynn W. Payne

Chief Management Strategist
Renaissance Strategies

Cissy Lennon

Distance Technology Program Manager for Aircraft Certification
Federal Aviation Administration

INTRODUCTION

Exercises constitute a large portion of the education and training classes and courses instructors conduct. They are the very essence of what instructors do in classrooms and laboratories. Many instructors and developers who create classroom instruction initially resist adapting their courses for delivery by a particular distance learning technology. After all, how could one possibly deliver their course at a distance? How could the exercises used in their traditional classroom be adapted for delivery by distance learning technologies and still be effective? Many quickly conclude it is not possible.

The objective of this chapter is to show that it is not only possible, but it is also done every day quite effectively by many different organizations, using many different distribution methods, or distance learning technologies, to deliver the instruction. The purpose of this chapter is to demonstrate how to adapt a number of instructional exercises for delivery by multiple distance learning technologies.

What Are Exercises?

Exercises are those activities conducted or directed by the instructor, by the instructor and learners, or by learners to help them obtain and retain a particular block of information. Exercises can be simple paper-and-pencil activities or complex simulations involving multi-million dollar simulators. The mental requirements of exercises can be very simple or extremely complex. Individual learners, groups of learners, or an entire class can perform exercises.

What Do Exercises Accomplish?

Different exercises satisfy different objectives. The results of exercises provide instructors with information about the following:

- whether learners have satisfied the objectives for the exercise
- where learners need corrective feedback, additional instruction, and additional practice
- parts of the instruction that need revision because they don't give learners the information they need.

Learners can use the results from an exercise to do the following:

- check their individual accomplishment of the objectives for that instructional unit
- compare their performance with that of their fellow learners.

Exercises may satisfy other objectives that aren't necessarily related to the content of the instructional unit. For example, group exercises can show instructors the following:

- which learners assume leadership roles in groups
- which learners are willing to follow others
- which learners work well with other learners in groups.

Individual exercises can show instructors which learners can follow directions and how well learners can work alone without the instructors' direct oversight.

COMPONENTS OF GOOD EXERCISES

Generally, all good exercises share the following basic components, regardless of their complexity, equipment requirements, and the number of learners involved:

- All exercises should have a definite beginning and a clear ending.
- Exercises should have a clear purpose, and learners should know what is expected of them. Instructors should tell learners the objective before the exercise, most of the time. There are a few exercises where the purpose is held until the end of the exercise, and learners are expected to determine the purpose as one of the objectives of the exercise. However, these types of exercises are fairly uncommon.
- Exercises should have directions explaining what learners are to do. The complexity and detail of the directions will vary depending on the complexity and purpose of the exercise. Directions should be complete, understandable by the learners, and in many cases, written down for referral during the exercise.
- After the exercise, there should be a feedback session in which learners get direct feedback about their performance.

In some instances, additional practice or another exercise that allows the learners to demonstrate achievement of the objective may follow this feedback.

ADAPTING EXERCISES FOR DELIVERY BY DISTANCE LEARNING TECHNOLOGIES

Instructional exercises include role playing, lectures, games, expert panels, practical exercises, team collaboration, readings, and simulations. It is possible to adapt each of these for delivery by teletraining, video teleconferencing, audio conferencing, CD-ROM, and the Internet or intranet. The sections that follow will provide the following:

- descriptions of each of the distance learning technologies
- examples of instructional exercises in traditional classes
- for each exercise, recommendations on how to adapt each exercise for delivery by each of the distance learning technologies.

DESCRIPTIONS OF TECHNOLOGIES

The following descriptions of distance learning technologies include either the term *synchronous* or the term *asynchronous,* both of which were described in chapter three. To review, with synchronous instructional delivery, all learners take instruction at the same time; with asynchronous instructional delivery, learners take the instruction at different times. Most distance learning technologies deliver instruction either synchronously or asynchronously. However, the Internet and intranet are capable of delivering instruction both synchronously and asynchronously, and in many instances, equally effectively.

Teletraining

Teletraining is synchronous two-way audio and one-way video instruction conducted with groups of learners. The learners can see and hear the instructor, but the instructor can only hear the learners, and learners can only hear one another. Some teletraining systems use a viewer response system that allows for instructors to collect data responses from each of them on preplanned objective-type questions.

Video Teleconferencing

Video teleconferencing is synchronous, two-way audio and two-way video instruction conducted with groups of learners. Learners can see and hear the instructor, the instructor can see and hear the learners, and learners can see and hear one another. Many video teleconferencing systems also allow each site to share graphic material with other sites.

Audio Conferencing

Two types of audio conferencing are under consideration in this chapter: audio teletraining and audiographics. Audio teletraining is two-way synchronous audio-only instruction for which learners usually receive their materials before the event. Audiographics is two-way synchronous audio with computer graphics sent to each participant's computer. Learners can see the instructor's graphic on their computer monitor. Some more advanced systems allow the instructor and learners to share computer graphics.

CD-ROM

CD-ROM is asynchronous, self-paced, interactive instruction conducted on a multimedia computer using video, sound, graphics, and animation. While a number of learners may be working on the same lesson, each learner is usually expected to work alone and at his or her own pace.

Internet or Intranet

Training over the Internet and intranet can take a variety of forms. Synchronous types of Internet and intranet courses can be very sophisticated and include two-way audio and two-way video, similar to video teleconferencing. Synchronous types of Internet or intranet courses can also be less sophisticated, such as online courses followed by scheduled chat rooms, where all class members and the instructor log on at the same time and carry on electronic discussions. Examples of asynchronous types of Internet and intranet courses are self-paced computer-based instruction that is similar to instruction delivered by CD-ROM, and online text-based courses.

ADAPTING INSTRUCTIONAL EXERCISES
Role Playing

The objective of role-playing exercises is to provide learners with opportunities to practice applying information and procedures they recently learned.

Resident Classroom Example. A learner is assigned the primary role of a flight inspector for the Federal Aviation Association and is attempting to gain admittance to the cockpit of a commercial airliner to do an en route cockpit crew inspection. The instructor plays the role of the pilot. Other learners play the roles of other cockpit crew members. The pilot (instructor) refuses to admit the FAA flight inspector because an airline employee will be occupying the jump seat, which is where the inspector sits during an inspection, in order to get to another work location. In this example, the learner practices attempting to gain admittance to the cockpit and informing the pilot of the potential consequences for refusing that admittance. At the conclusion of the exercise, the instructor would lead a discussion about what happened during the role play. This feedback session should include what was good, areas for improvement related to the role-play exercise, and any emphasis the instructor may want to place on a certain area or procedure.

Teletraining Example. If remote broadcast capability is technically possible, the crew side of the role play can be conducted in an aircraft or simulator with on-site instructors assigned to play the roles of pilot and co-pilot. A simulated scenario that is just as effective is to broadcast directly from the studio with the crew wearing official-looking jackets or hats to make them look like pilot and co-pilot. The learner who plays the role of the FAA flight inspector would communicate with the cockpit crew using the system's voice capability, but only the crew would be projected on the TV monitor. For an additional sense of reality, when the flight inspector presents his credentials to the cockpit crew, the on-camera participants can "pretend" receipt by having someone off camera hand them an official-looking identification card. Even with only one-way video capability, the role play can be accomplished quite effectively. In this environment, the role play progresses much as it would in a resident classroom, including the essential feedback session at the end.

Video Teleconferencing Example. The addition of two-way video with two-way audio allows an even more realistic exchange in the role play. All learners would then view both the pilot and cockpit crew and the flight inspector roles on the TV monitor. Since the players are at different locations and learners can't see them at the same time, a simulated exchange of documentation can be planned ahead of time, with an unseen extra at the instructor's location handing over identification documentation to the "pilot." The role play and feedback would be basically what they are in a resident classroom.

Audio Conferencing Example. In an audio teletraining or an audiographics environment, participants hear the voices of the pilot and the flight inspector, but they don't get visual images. Instructors can expand the method to include a narrator who would set the context for the en route cockpit inspection for all of the listeners. Either way, the role play in this environment would progress much the same as it would in a resident classroom.

CD-ROM Example. For CD-ROM, it would be necessary to create a video scenario in which, at critical points, the audio or video asks learners to make a choice about the inspector's next step in the en route cockpit crew inspection process. The learners' responses trigger the next video scenario that they'll see. After learners view the next scenario, they get feedback, with branching and remedial training as needed, about whether or not each response is correct. The learner would work through the scenario by making a series of decisions and seeing the results of those decisions depicted in the video clip scenarios. At the end of the lesson, an evaluation provides the learner with further feedback about how well he or she did as the flight inspector in the scenario and which decisions were handled most appropriately. Remedial instruction should be offered for any inappropriate choices. Feedback during the program is used as a teaching point about why the choice was correct or incorrect, whereas feedback at the end summarizes the learners' performance and offers additional remedial information for those areas where incorrect choices were made.

Internet or Intranet Example. In an asynchronous mode, the role play would be adapted the same as it would for delivery by CD-ROM. It is simply computer-based instruction that is delivered to the learner's computer over the Internet or intranet. In a synchronous mode, the role play would be adapted the same as for delivery by video teleconferencing, with one noticeable exception: The learner would be alone at a computer instead of in a group using a video teleconference system. However, the system would still provide two-way audio and two-way video capability for the role play. Whether delivered in an asynchronous or a synchronous mode, a feedback session would need to be provided, as it would using either CD-ROM or video teleconferencing.

Lectures

The objective of a lecture is to communicate information and ideas to the learners. Instructors' voice, hand movements, body movement, facial expressions, and eye contact with learners can help or hinder this communication. Good lectures feel like a spontaneous conversation that an instructor has with each individual learner.

⚌ Resident Classroom Example. The instructor's task is to provide the learners with information about record keeping as it relates to preparing to assist an individual with an audit of his federal income tax return. The instructor organizes the delivery of the information, uses a conversational tone, incorporates stories to illustrate points, maintains eye contact with learners, and uses movement to gain and hold attention, emphasize a point, or start a new topic. A good strategy for a lecture is to do the following:

- As an introduction, tell the learners what you are going to tell them.
- Present the lecture.
- As a summary, tell the learners what you told them.
- Use graphics for providing an outline of the lecture and to summarize key points during the lecture.
- Allow time at the end of the lecture for learners to ask questions so they can clarify their understanding of the information and ideas presented.

◧ Teletraining Example. The same basic principles for delivering a lecture in a resident classroom apply to lectures using teletraining. In the teletraining environment, however, it is strongly recommended that graphics be developed to support and augment the lecture. If converting an existing lecture for delivery by teletraining, the graphics will need to meet the principles of good graphic design for television. Also, learner attention can be maintained by frequently changing camera angles when showing the instructor and by switching to graphic support material often to support the instructor's content. Care should be taken in managing time to ensure that learners have time after the lecture to ask questions.

Video Teleconferencing Example. The principles are basically the same as they were with teletraining. Learner attention can be maintained by frequently switching between the instructor and graphic support. One noticeable difference between teletraining and video teleconferencing is that in this format the instructor will be able to see learners as they ask questions in order to clarify their understanding of the information and ideas presented.

Audio Conferencing Example. With audio teletraining, an outline of the lecture should be included in the learner materials sent to the learners prior to the start of the course. The instructor should deliver the lecture in much the same manner as he or she would in the teletraining environment because the instructor can't see the learners. Audiographic technology can also effectively deliver lectures in a manner similar to that in a teletraining environment. Graphics can be shown to the learners during the lecture, and the instructor can change them at the appropriate time. As with teletraining, graphics will need to meet good graphic design principles. With both types of audio conferencing, learners should have time to ask questions.

CD-ROM Example. Although CD-ROMs can deliver lectures, instructors should take care to ensure that these lectures are kept short and that they don't overuse them. Instructors should follow lectures with some other exercise to allow the learners to verify that they learned the material. A lecture in this environment should be short, concise, and to the point. It is recommended that the audio component presents the lectures while the video component shows accompanying graphics, video clips, or animations. Learners who view the "lecturette" should then receive some type of exercise to demonstrate they've mastered the information and ideas in it. Review questions, practical exercises, and simulations are good exercises for this purpose.

Internet or Intranet Example. The lecture can be effectively delivered in an asynchronous format over the Internet or intranet in a manner similar to that for the CD-ROM. It is recommended that learners download the lesson onto the hard drive of their computer to speed up the running of the program.

Lectures developed to be conducted synchronously would be conducted like those for video teleconferencing. As with video teleconferencing, the exercise should conclude with time allotted for learners to ask questions.

Games

Games are to reinforce and review course information by allowing learners to apply what they have learned.

Resident Classroom Example. The game is patterned after the *Jeopardy* game show on television. (To avoid copyright issues, do not use the *Jeopardy* logo, music, or copy design.) The purpose of this game is to review a block of instruction before an exam. The game consists of developing several overall subject categories and within each category developing a number of review questions and answers, with each item worth a varying number of points. Learners are divided into teams. Each team takes turns answering questions, and each team member takes turns answering questions. A team member chooses a category for a certain number of points, and the instructor gives the "answer." The team must correctly identify the "question" to receive credit for the points assigned to that item. For example, if the instructor says, "the address of a homepage on the World Wide Web," a learner may say, "What is a uniform resource locator?" Each team takes its turn until all categories have been taken. Point totals are tallied for each team, and the team having the highest score is acclaimed the winner. At the end of the game, the instructor allows time for questions from learners to ensure they understand any items that may have been answered incorrectly during the game.

This game can be played in an electronic or a nonelectronic format. In the nonelectronic format, the instructor uses an overhead projector to show the game board with categories and point values, and he or she manually crosses out categories as learners use them. Teams take turns choosing items, and the instructor reads them aloud. The instructor also keeps score. In the electronic form, the instructor programs the game on a computer. The scores are tallied automatically using a separate menu on the computer.

Teletraining Example. It is probably most efficiently done using electronically generated computer images projected on the TV monitor. This format resembles the television game show version. The instructor can run the game using a mouse to click on the categories and items, occasionally recapping the scores by projecting the electronic scoring screen. A site competition can be established with each site acting as a team. Item choices should be rotated between sites. The instructor would read the answer for each category selected, and a team member would provide the correct question.

The game can also be run in the nonelectronic format, using the document camera to project the game board.

In both the electronic and nonelectronic formats, the game in a teletraining system would progress in a similar manner to that in a resident classroom, and instructors would leave time for learners to ask questions.

Video Teleconferencing Example. In this format, as in teletraining, the game could be run electronically or nonelectronically. In either case, it would have the advantage that all participants would be able to see each other as they select categories and respond. It could evolve into a lively and competitive exercise. Because most videoconferencing systems are voice-activated, care must be taken to plan for an orderly rotation of the questions to prevent the loudest site from taking control.

In both the electronic and nonelectronic formats, the game would be similar to that in a resident classroom. Here, too, instructors should allow time for learners to ask questions.

Audio Conferencing Example. To use audio teletraining for conducting the game, before the course, instructors should send learners a paper copy of the game board with categories and point values. Instructors should tell learners to mark off categories as they are used.

To use audiographics for conducting the game, the computer image of the game board should be sent to the learners using the graphic capability. As the instructor uses and marks off each category on the game board, he or she should send an updated image to the learners.

Learners in both the audio teletraining and the audiographics environments may be at individual telephones or workstations rather than in groups, so the team approach may not be appropriate. If this is the case, instructors should conduct the game with individual learners rather than teams. This arrangement may require more time for the game because the instructor will need to make sure that all learners get the opportunity to play. One possible strategy could be to allow a pre-selected set of three individuals to play together and declare a winner at that point. Then, continue the game with three different individuals. Other learners should pay attention and answer the questions mentally. The instructor will need to watch the time to ensure that sufficient time is available at the end of the game for questions.

CD-ROM Example. Using a CD-ROM to deliver the game requires an electronic format, with automatic scoring. The competitiveness of playing against other players or on a team is lost with this distribution method. Players would play alone and evaluate their own knowledge level on the basis of how well they perform. At the end of the game, learners should be provided with a performance review. This review should summarize how well the learner did, such as saying, "You got 90 percent correct." This review should also detail any areas in which learners missed questions and provide those learners with the option of remedial instruction in each of those areas.

Internet or Intranet Example. The game can be conducted asynchronously over the Internet or intranet in a manner similar to that of the CD-ROM game. Learners should download the game from the Internet or intranet onto the hard drive on their computer to speed up the responsiveness of the game.

The game can also be conducted in the asynchronous format over the Internet or intranet using the same strategies as those for video teleconferencing. The instructor must allow time for learners to ask questions.

Expert Panel

The objective of an expert panel exercise is to provide learners with the opportunity to ask specific questions to experts in a given area. The learners have the opportunity to learn from the experience of the panel members and to get ideas about dealing with specific issues.

Resident Classroom Example. In a class on stock market investing, the instructor uses an expert panel exercise to expose the learners to a variety of successful investment strategies and to provide the learners with opportunities for interaction with the experts. The instructor invites several professional investment counselors—the experts—to the class to give their view of current stock market conditions and to describe the investment strategies they are using under these conditions. The instructor seats the investment counselors in front of the class. They will each speak for a set amount of time, giving their view of current market conditions and the investment strategies they are using. After the last expert speaks, the instructor serves as the moderator while learners pose questions to the experts. After the session has ended and the experts have departed, the instructor should provide a summary of the event. This summary should include what the learners should have learned from the experts, and it should provide learners with the opportunity to ask questions about anything that occurred during the expert panel session.

Teletraining Example. The investment counselors can be brought in to the broadcast facility to make their presentations on camera and to answer questions from learners calling in from remote locations. The exercise would be similar to that in a resident classroom, although instructors and counselors cannot see the learners with hands raised to ask questions. Because audio systems used with some teletraining courses allow for instantaneous responses from learners, the instructor must exercise control as the moderator during the question and answer period to ensure an orderly exchange between the learners and the expert panelists. Just as in the resident classroom, the instructor should summarize the event and give the learners an opportunity to ask questions.

With some teletraining systems, it would be possible for expert panelists who couldn't attend in person to participate in the broadcast. However, only their voice would be heard. Instructors could personalize their participation by using their photographs. The photo of an expert would be put under a document camera and projected on the monitor while he or she is talking. In this scenario, experts would take turns calling in to participate, making their presentations and answering learners' questions one at a time. After the last expert's call, the instructor would present the summary and take learners' questions.

▤ Video Teleconferencing Example. Expert panels conducted via video teleconferencing are much like those conducted using teletraining, with the instructors serving as hosts and moderators during the presentations and panelists' questions, and then presenting final summaries and taking questions. Because most video teleconferencing systems are voice activated, it is imperative that the instructor establish a protocol for learners to minimize interruptions during the presentations and the question and answer period.

It is possible for one or more panelists to participate from a video teleconferencing site at a different location from the instructor. The two-way audio and two-way video capability of the video teleconferencing system allow all sites to see and hear whoever is speaking. This will allow the experts to present from their own location and be seen and heard, and for the experts to see and hear learners when asking questions. The instructor's role as moderator is critical to the orderly and timely presentations by the experts as well as the question and answer session between the experts and the learners.

Audio Conferencing Example. Expert panel discussions can be conducted using either audio teletraining or audiographics. Be aware that because learners won't be able to see the experts, some of the spontaneity of the event is lost and it may hold less interest for the learners. However, there is still merit in using the technology to expose the learners to knowledgeable authorities for the information they possess.

As with the other distance learning technologies, it is important that the instructor serve as moderator, provide a summary, and give learners a chance to ask questions.

CD-ROM Example. CD-ROM technology can provide expert panel discussions for individual learners through development of video clips of experts giving an overview of their thoughts on stock market investment strategies and pressing them onto the CD-ROM. Due to the time lag involved in making and distributing CD-ROMs, the focus of the experts' presentations would need to be on more generic investment issues and strategies rather than presentations on current market conditions. One strategy that could be used to help make the presentation more interactive would be for the program to start with a series of short video clips from three or four experts. The learner could be presented with a menu of specific topics. As the learner selects a particular topic, a video clip of one of the experts could present the information. A different strategy could provide the learner with practice selecting a particular investment strategy to meet a given market situation. As the learner makes a selection, the expert recommending that strategy could provide feedback as to whether the learner's selection was an appropriate one. The program should provide a summary of those video clips viewed by the learner, independent of the strategy used.

⬛ **Internet or Intranet Example.** Expert panel exercises can be effectively delivered using the Internet or intranet. An asynchronous exercise would be conducted in much the same manner as that using CD-ROM technology. If the expert panelists consent, it is possible for learners to send them follow-up questions via email. If a chat room was established for the class, all learners and the instructor could share and discuss the questions and answers.

If the exercise is developed to be synchronous, it would be conducted in much the same manner as that of video teleconferencing. Again, if the expert panelists consent, it would be possible for learners to send them questions via email. Here, too, a chat room would benefit all the learners and the instructor.

Practical Exercise

The objective of a practical exercise is to provide learners with the opportunity to apply what they have learned to a given situation or a series of situations.

⬛ **Resident Classroom Example.** After receiving a lesson on how to create visuals that are appropriate for broadcast over instructional television, the learners complete an exercise to reinforce and review the principles of good visual design for creating instructional television graphics. In this exercise, learners are given a poorly designed graphic and asked to recreate it using the guidelines learned in the lesson. This exercise can be done in either an electronic version, using a computer with appropriate graphic software, or in a manual version, using a paper copy and colored pencils. After the learners have completed the exercise, the instructor should randomly call on them to show their corrected graphic to the class. Learners should explain why they made the changes they did and, as much as possible, relate their corrections to the principles of good graphic design. After learners' have shown their graphics, the instructor should summarize the exercise and lead the class in a discussion of the principles of good graphic design.

Teletraining Example. After receiving a lesson on how to create visuals that are appropriate for broadcast over instructional television, the instructor should give the learners a poorly designed visual and ask them to use principles of good graphic design to improve it. Learners would send the finished visuals to the instructor by fax for evaluation and to share them with the entire class. If large groups of learners are at the remote receive sites, each site might fax in one or two drawings rather than all drawings. Although color choices will be lost because the faxes will show up in black and white, participants can discuss other areas of the design. Selected visuals can be put on the document camera and broadcast to all sites for discussion. Learners should explain their changes as their graphic is broadcast. As with the classroom example, the instructor should conclude the exercise by summarizing it and leading a discussion of the principles of good graphic design.

Video Teleconferencing Example. With two-way audio and two-way video capabilities of video teleconferencing, this exercise could be conducted in much the same manner as in a resident classroom. The instructor would call on learners to project their corrected graphic for discussion and feedback from the instructor and other learners.

Audio Conferencing Example. The exercise would have to be conducted somewhat differently for audioteletraining than for audiographics. Learners would have to receive a copy of a poorly designed graphic in the learner course materials they get before the class begins. Learners would be asked to develop an improved graphic and fax the design back to the instructor for a verbal evaluation. Because there is no visual component with audio teletraining, the instructor would have to generalize about which principles the class as a whole applied correctly, didn't apply correctly, or didn't apply at all. Also, colors would have to be discussed rather than displayed.

Because of the visual component, this practical exercise can be conducted more effectively using audiographics than audio teletraining. Again, learners would receive a copy of a poorly designed graphic with their course materials, and they would have to develop an improved graphic and fax the design back to the instructor. The audiographic system should allow the instructor to display the corrected graphics for all learners to see. As their graphic is displayed, learners would describe how they corrected the graphic and the principles of good graphic design that guided their decisions. Many audiographic systems would allow the instructor to "draw" on the poorly designed visual using a special pen and an interaction tablet. The instructor would be able to annotate key areas, show deficiencies, and illustrate how to improve each learner graphic shown. With both audio conferencing methods, the exercise would conclude with the instructor's summary and a discussion of the principles of good graphic design.

CD-ROM Example. With CD-ROM, learners would first view instruction using text or audio and video about how to develop visuals for television and how to apply the principles of good graphic design. Learners could then view and evaluate examples of poorly designed graphics. On the basis of their responses, they might get remedial training with reviews of the improperly applied principle of good graphic design or branch to other examples. In another scenario, learners could be shown a series of poorly designed examples. For each poorly designed example, the learner would be shown four to six corrected versions from which to select the best version. Again, branching and remedial training could be provided on the basis of their responses. At the conclusion of the exercise, learners would receive a summary of their performance as well as a review of the principles of good graphic design.

Internet or Intranet Example. An asynchronous exercise via the Internet or intranet would be conducted in much the same manner as one using CD-ROM technology. The exercise could be modified to include an example of a poorly designed graphic. The learner would revise that example on the computer, explain the changes related to the principles of good graphic design, and send it to the instructor via email. The instructor would evaluate and comment on the graphic and return it to the learner.

If the exercise is developed to be conducted synchronously, it would be conducted in much the same manner as the one for video teleconferencing. That is, learners would display their corrected version of the graphic, explaining why they made their corrections, and receiving feedback from the instructor or other learners. As with video teleconferencing, the exercise would conclude with the instructor's summary of the exercise and a discussion of the principles of good graphic design.

Team Collaboration

Team collaborations are groups of learners who work on a specific exercise or a series of exercises to accomplish a specific learning outcome. The team may be disbanded after one exercise, or it can stay together for an entire course.

⊞ Resident Classroom Example. Learners in the class divide into teams of equal number. The instructor gives each team the assignment to develop a marketing strategy for a given business scenario. Each team gets background information about the company and its products and services. The instructor serves as the source for historical information and current competitive market conditions. In this example, a 100-year-old family-owned chocolate candy business in downtown Baltimore has engaged the team to determine whether or not the company should expand its production capabilities and modify its packaging and its target market. The team must collect the appropriate data for decision making based on a SWOT—strengths, weaknesses, opportunities, and threats—analysis and environmental analysis. Each team must agree on a marketing strategy and present it to the class. At the conclusion of the exercise, the instructor will lead the class in a discussion covering the following:

- what information each team used for the decision making
- where the information was obtained
- how each team came to agreement.

Teletraining Example. Just as learners at the resident classroom site band into teams, learners at each receive site location form into teams. Teams may transmit their questions to the instructor through the system's audio capability, and the questions may be augmented with visuals using the TV monitor. Pictures and graphics that the instructor prepared may assist the learners in visualizing their given scenarios, thus inspiring both creative and analytical thinking processes. In this environment, the team collaboration progresses much as it would in a resident classroom, to include the team's presentation of its selected marketing strategy and the instructor-led discussion at the end.

Video Teleconferencing Example. With two-way video and two-way audio, instructors can observe the team collaboration process in the same manner as they would in a resident classroom. This process can be helpful when at least one of the objectives is the development of team leadership or teamwork. There is no additional benefit to the learners unless the instructor has to intervene to solve a team-related problem. The team's presentation and the class discussion follow the same format as in the other examples.

Audio Conferencing Example. The instructor's limited role in a team collaboration exercise does not inhibit the process in this voice-only environment. The simpler the background information the instructor supplies, the less the instructor and learners have to interact. In audio teletraining and audiographic environments, learners are divided into teams on the basis of their physical location. The ability this method gives learners to hear one another's questions and responses may assist teams in their analytical processes. The format for the team's presentation and class discussion is the same as in the other examples.

⊙ **CD-ROM Example.** This method of delivery can provide for team collaboration, but it is not ideal. An individual would interact with other team members who are built into preprogrammed pathways of the CD-ROM. Discussion is not suppressed, but it is restricted to preprogrammed responses. Learners select options and view the results based on the individual input. Any discussion is provided by the preprogrammed analysis on the CD-ROM. Learners can read why certain results occurred, but they don't have the opportunity to experience group dynamics in person.

⬛ **Internet or Intranet Example.** In an asynchronous mode, the team collaboration would be introduced the same as it would for delivery by CD-ROM. In a synchronous mode, two-way audio and two-way video are available to the learner, with the difference being that team members are physically at different locations. Discussion among team members is limited only by transmission delays from the various technologies of the computers in use. Team dynamics can be experienced with the additional assistance of online search capabilities during the team exercise. One or more team members may search the Net during the team discussions. This format does not require instructor intervention because the information for each scenario is on a given Website. Each team would develop a marketing strategy, present it to the class, and receive feedback from the instructor and other learners. The instructor should lead a discussion at the end to summarize the exercise.

Reading

Reading exercises can meet several objectives. They can provide the following:

- background material for learners who need to review or acquire skills or knowledge to succeed in class
- basic reading essential to the course
- in-depth reading for learners who wish to delve deeper into particular subject areas.

Resident Classroom Example. The instructor would specify reading assignments prior to discussion of the material in class. In a management class, learners would read *Theory X: The Traditional View of Direction and Control* and *Theory Y: The Integration of Individual and Organizational Goals,* by Douglas McGregor, before receiving a lecture on management styles. This material would provide the learners with a historical reference point and baseline information to assist them in applying the lecture content to current situations and conditions. An instructor may choose learners at random to defend one theory or the other. This allows learners who have all read the same material to exercise creative thinking in determining when each of the theories would be appropriate. Such challenges often do not exist when the learner simply reads the material and is not asked to analyze, apply, support, or defend the information and ideas read.

Teletraining Example. The reading exercises applicable to a resident classroom are appropriate with teletraining. In addition, with teletraining, learners at various locations can interact with the instructor as well as with other learners. The instructor may display selected portions of the readings on the monitor to stimulate discussion.

Video Teleconferencing Example. Two-way video can provide an animated discussion of the assigned readings. The examples applicable in a resident classroom apply here as well.

Audio Conferencing Example. Reading assignments without discussion obviously do not require any particular technology. Instructors will occasionally assign supplemental reading when contact time is limited, but the content is necessary for complete comprehension of course material. With audio conferencing, discussion of the controversial Theory X and Theory Y material may assist the learners in their critical thinking skills. Opposing viewpoints and multiple scenarios can provide a meaningful foundation for understanding management theory.

⊙ **CD-ROM Example.** When learners don't have a group with which to discuss the opposing theories of management, the CD-ROM can be effective. After a learner reads the assigned material, the CD-ROM plays the role of challenger by running video clips that contain work situations where managers use the different theories of management and require the learner to respond to questions about the video scenarios in terms of each management theory. This technology allows the learner to read about the theories, then see the theories acted out. It should have an end-of-lesson summary so learners can verify their learning.

◈ **Internet or Intranet Example.** In an asynchronous mode, the reading discussion would be similar to the activity utilizing CD-ROM. The exercise is based on the reading material, but learners respond to computer-based instruction that is run on the Internet or intranet. It is recommended that learners download the lesson to their computer in order to speed up the running of the program. Also, an end-of-lesson summary should be provided to allow the learner to verify their learning.

A synchronous mode of Internet or intranet delivery allows learners to discuss management theory as they would using video teleconferencing. The instructor may have to facilitate or moderate to ensure that the learners stay on track.

Simulation

The use of simulation represents a way for organizations to gain strategic advantage. Learners participate in the enactment of procedures impossible or unlikely in the real world because of logistics, expense, or safety concerns. Simulation is an enabling technology that lets organizations take risks, discover engineering end results, and find the best implementation scenarios while quantifying specific savings and changes. Simulations allow learners to apply what they have learned in a real-world environment, complete with real-world consequences of their actions and decisions.

Resident Classroom Example. It is generally preferred that learners attending law enforcement training be able to identify friend from foe before they are issued real bullets for their weapons. "Oops!" is not a welcome response when weapons have been drawn and fired. Simulations give learners the opportunity to recognize a target before shooting, and then to shoot for effect or deadly force. In this simulation, there is a realistic environment made of plywood or cardboard, either indoors or outdoors, and there are pop-up targets. Learners are asked to react using weapons loaded with blanks according to a given scenario. They can practice identifying friend or foe and time themselves during the recognition process. This exercise helps to ensure that innocent people are not injured and that the bad guys don't get away. This exercise can be repeated many times by moving the targets and buildings around. Time needs to be allowed at the end of the exercise for the instructor to lead a discussion about how learners made decisions about whether to fire or not fire.

Teletraining Example. A simulation can be effectively created in the broadcast studio using learner response systems to improve recognition and eye-hand coordination. The scenario is actually acted out in the studio either with real people entering the viewing area or with a computer-generated simulation that appears on the screen. As subjects enter the viewing area, or pop up, the learners must physically react by pushing the go or no-go response buttons. When real actors are used, additional theatrics such as fake blood and sounds can enhance the realism. As would be done in a resident classroom, time should be provided at the end of the exercise for an instructor-led discussion.

Video Teleconferencing Example. Two-way video with two-way audio allows for additional interaction between the officers and the offenders or private citizens. No one actually gets shot, but the learners' emotional reactions and dialogue can be quite realistic and useful in training. Learners at all sites can see each others' facial expressions, body language, and actions, and they can react to what they see one another do as well as what they say. Officers use rubber guns with audio-firing mechanisms, and the targets react accordingly when shot. Here, too, the instructor would lead a discussion.

Audio Conferencing Example. Audio-only delivery technologies are not as effective as those with video. Without visuals, the simulation takes place as if it were in the dark. Voice commands are used to encourage the targets to identify themselves audibly. The officers then use an audio response system to simulate firing a weapon. The ensuing sound effects can be quite realistic.

With audiographics, the instructor can send a graphic similar to a pop-up target along with the voices. Individual learners can take turns deciding whether or not to fire, based upon the graphic on their computer screens. Discussions should follow both the audio conference methods.

CD-ROM Example. The CD-ROM method uses a video scenario that functions like a video game with a joystick. Targets appear from around corners, requiring the officer using the CD-ROM to make an instant identification and choose whether or not to fire. The computer can keep track of how long it took for the officer to make a decision to fire and how many correct and incorrect hits were made. At the end of the simulation, the computer provides the learner with a summary score and offers remedial instruction in those areas where the learner made incorrect decisions.

Internet or Intranet Example. The Internet or intranet simulation in an asynchronous mode would provide computer-based instruction similar to that of the CD-ROM exercise. The officer would respond with a joystick to targets appearing on the screen.

In the synchronous mode, the lesson would be similar to the one using video teleconferencing. Targets would appear on the screen from remote locations, and the officers would react with rubber guns and audio for gun shots. Discussions should follow both.

SUMMARY

Exercises should be an integral part of every instructional event, and one of the requirements of effective exercises is that they be interactive. While it has been well documented that interactivity relevant to the subject matter enhances learning, all too often we hear a trainer faced with transitioning to distance learning say, "I don't have time for interaction," "I've got too much to cover," or "I don't know how to interact when learners aren't in the room with me." Organizations are turning more frequently to technology-delivered training when they look for ways to reduce the cost of training employees, to increase access to training opportunities for employees, and to provide just-in-time training for employees. As a result, new and innovative ways of thinking need to be implemented that are relevant for distance learning.

This chapter illustrated that instructors can effectively adapt many of the exercises they use in resident classroom environments to one of the popular distance learning technologies, such as teletraining, video teleconferencing, CD-ROM, audio conferencing, and the Internet or intranet. The key to successfully adapting an exercise for a given technology is first to understand the capabilities and limitations of each technology and then to creatively use those capabilities and limitations to conduct the exercise to its maximum effectiveness. When done properly, learners will find such exercises challenging and exciting opportunities to demonstrate their learning.

THE AUTHOR

Hank Payne is director of the Office of Training and Education, Occupational Safety and Health Administration (OSHA), U.S. Department of Labor. He is responsible for training federal and state compliance officers, state consultants, employers, and workers on the recognition, identification, and abatement of hazardous and unsafe conditions in the workplace. He is responsible for the conduct of OSHA courses by the OSHA Training Institute (OTI), administration of the Susan Harwood Training Grant Program, and the development of outreach material. Payne also oversees the OTI Education Centers, which offer OSHA-developed courses primarily for other federal agency employees, employers, and workers.

Payne worked for the Federal Aviation Administration (FAA) from 1991 to 1998, where he served as manager of its distance learning program. He was directly responsible for the FAA's Interactive Video Teletraining Program, a satellite-delivered technical training program. He was also directly responsible for the design of an innovative approach to studio design, which reduced the number of people required for a satellite broadcast from eight to 12 down to one.

Payne is past-president of the Federal Government Distance Learning Association, a chapter of the U.S. Distance Learning Association. He is on the board of directors of the U.S. Distance Learning Association and president of the Government Alliance for Training and Education.

Lynn W. Payne has extensive experience in the areas of distance learning, program planning, resource management, strategic planning, total quality management, and marketing strategies. She currently is a consultant for Renaissance Strategies, a company near Chicago specializing in the integration of new technologies and initiatives for forward-thinking organizations.

Her experience includes teaching marketing and management courses at Langston University, serving as a member of the Board of Advisors for the Oklahoma Quality Award Foundation, providing training and leadership for state examiners, and being a regional judge for the Association of Quality and Participation regional team competitions and a judge for the Oklahoma Quality Award Foundation. Payne served as contract manager for General Electric's Government Engineering and Management Services Division, and as a finance officer for the U.S. Army as Chief of Resource Management for the Training Technology Agency.

She holds a B.S. in business administration from James Madison University, an M.B.A. in management from Golden Gate University, a Ph.D. in business management from LaSalle University, and a Ph.D. in adult and higher education from the University of Oklahoma, where she is a member of the Honor Society Phi Kappa Phi.

Cissy Lennon serves as the distance technology program manager for the Federal Aviation Association's Aircraft Certification Service. Aircraft Certification's primary distance learning focus has been on the use of interactive video teletraining (IVT) to accomplish training in specialized technical areas. Prior to this position, Lennon served as the FAA's IVT operations manager and as the program manager for correspondence study. She was one of the primary developers of the FAA's IVT Skills Course, a five-day hands-on course that prepares instructors and developers for the IVT arena. She has also taught train-the-trainer courses for several years.

Lennon has a B.A. in psychology from the University of Miami, an M.A. in educational research from the University of Pittsburgh, an M.Ed. in counseling psychology from the University of Central Oklahoma, and a Ph.D. in adult education from the University of Oklahoma. She is an officer of the Federal Government Distance Learning Association.

Section 3:

Model Exercises in Distance Learning

Introduction to Chapters 8, 9, and 10

Case Studies and Lessons Learned

It's always helpful to see how the pros have achieved excellence in any area that is important to us. How they have created effective and enjoyable interactivity exercises is no exception. Because many internal trainers are starting to develop distance learning courses in-house, it becomes critical to have a foundation for making the transition to those on-site exercises. If you should need the support of an outside vendor, at least you can have a jump start by seeing how other successful distance learning developers have created excellent, effective exercises. The three chapters that follow provide you with descriptions of transitions to three different distribution methods. Sharon G. Fisher and Will S. Peratino describe the move to training on the Internet at the U.S. Department of Defense's Defense Acquisition University. In chapter 9, Sue Faust explains how a unit of the University of Wisconsin-Extension introduced a course using audiographics conferencing. In the final chapter in the case study, Bruce E. Dewey describes the introduction of video teleconferencing for a unit of the Public Service Commission of Wisconsin. There are advantages and disadvantages to each of the methods in how and how effectively they enable the learners to interact with the instructor.

Chapter 8

Creating Interactivity on the Web: A DoD Case Study

Sharon G. Fisher

Vice President
Human Technology

Will S. Peratino

Director of Distance Learning
Defense Acquisition University

INTRODUCTION

A Web-based learning environment opens many new doors to instructional designers. At the same time, instructional designers must use new design concepts to foster interactivity in a Web-based learning environment. This case study presents the authors' experience in designing interactions in a Web-based learning environment at the U.S. Department of Defense's Defense Acquisition University (DAU). DAU provides education and training to more than 400,000 Department of Defense (DoD) employees worldwide. Web-based training combined with other distance learning technologies is becoming the university's preferred mode of training delivery of the majority of its 70 courses.

INSTRUCTIONAL METHODOLOGY: GROUP DISCUSSIONS

In a traditional classroom setting, students comment that they learn a lot through the exchange of ideas and experiences with other students. Table 8.1 describes some alternative methods DAU has developed for fostering this type of interaction in a Web-based learning environment and some of the things it considered during development.

Table 8.1. Approaches that foster group discussions.

DAU's Web Approach	Considerations and Lessons Learned
Course directors may elect to offer both synchronous and asynchronous forums for student exchange. Selected courses augment the Web instruction with scheduled teleconferences or video teletraining sessions.	Because most students are taking courses while on the job, DAU students prefer asynchronous Web communication modes. In courses where participation in asynchronous discussions is not mandatory, faculty members must encourage students to use this learning tool. The system sent automated email messages at the end of selected lessons suggesting that students participate in a specific forum. Faculty members must monitor communication forums to ensure the accuracy of the information being exchanged among students and to organize the discussions into logical trends. Additional software (or plug-ins) may need to be installed on the students' computers in order for the communication forums to work properly.

INSTRUCTIONAL METHODOLOGY: DISCUSSION QUESTIONS

In a classroom setting, discussion questions help students relate the content to their individual work settings and experiences. Table 8.2 shows DAU's approach and what the authors had to consider in designing the lessons.

Table 8.2. DAU's approach to discussion questions.

DAU's Web Approach	Considerations and Lessons Learned
In several courses, DAU has created characters that appear in each lesson. The characters represent cross-functional team members. A discussion question is posed. The student answers the question and then compares his or her response to the answers that the virtual team members provide.	Before beginning the lesson storyboards, identify all the characters you may need to present the different work experiences and viewpoints of your target population. Ideally, the students should be able to identify with one of the characters or feel as if they have met a person like the character in the workplace.
In another exercise, students are provided background on a problem. Next, the students are told that other team members have additional information on the situation. Students are encouraged to click on the different team members to review their points of view. Students are given feedback on their answers and the process they used to collaborate with their virtual team members.	Use the characters to tell a story. It is easier to remember a fact that is part of a story than a discrete piece of information. Caution: Don't make the story so complex that it requires the students to learn extraneous details.
	Use the characters to provide feedback on exercises where there is no definite correct response.
	Be consistent with your characters across lessons. This is especially important if multiple writers are developing lessons.

Figure 8.1 shows how DAU course designers used characters to engage students in the learning process. One screen displays all of the characters and requests that the student click on each team member to learn more. The other screens show how the students then interact with the selected character.

Students click on team members to learn more.

INSTRUCTIONAL METHODOLOGY: WORK SIMULATIONS

Simulating the work tasks is a key to promoting task transfer. The Web environment allows varying levels of work simulations. Table 8.3 shows DAU's approach to simulations and what it considered to achieve the results.

Figure 8.2 shows instructional exercises that closely resemble the kind of work students will perform. The simulated email and the

Figure 8.1. On-screen displays to engage students.

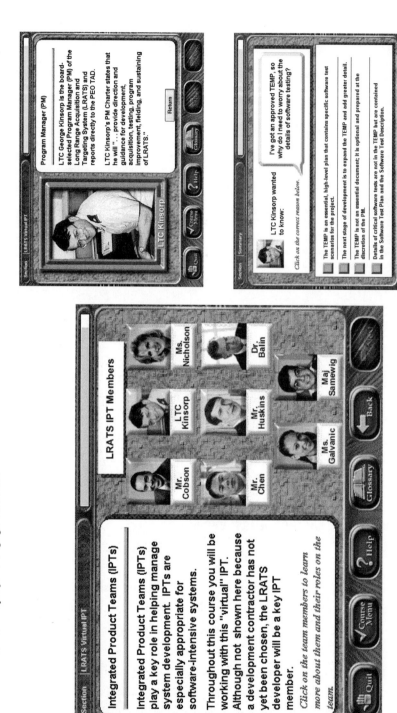

Table 8.3. DAU's approach to work simulation exercises.

DAU's Web Approach	Considerations and Lessons Learned
The primary job tasks DAU students perform involve the analysis of information and decision making. DAU has created several different types of work simulation exercises including: • a simulated email system through which students answer email messages that require them to make decisions • an in-basket that assigns students items to review and act on • sample data charts that require students to identify trends and select recommended courses of action.	Students were favorable toward the use of the office metaphor interface. However, students need instructions on how to navigate within the interface. Using a highly graphical interface over the Internet requires that students install a plug-in and download the graphics to their computers. Approximately 20 percent of the DAU students require help desk support to complete the required set-up process. A help desk is highly recommended if your course requires any type of set-up process.

chart require students to make the kind of choices they will face on the job.

INSTRUCTIONAL METHODOLOGY: GAMING

Games can help to motivate students to master lower-level knowledge objectives. One of DAU's approaches, described in table 8.4, is to use games on the Web to teach the many acronyms in use at the DoD. Figure 8.3 shows one of the pages in that game, the House of Cards.

INSTRUCTIONAL METHODOLOGY: TESTING

A combination of Internet and database technologies enables students to use testing as a learning activity and opportunity for individualized coaching. A summary of DAU's approach to testing and the instructional designers' considerations appears in table 8.5. The screen captures in figure 8.4 show two test questions and part of a status report.

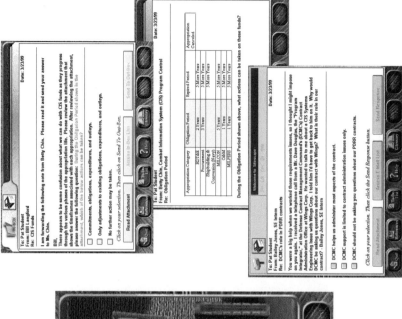

Figure 8.2. Instructional exercises that resemble work.

Table 8.4. DAU's approach to games.

DAU's Web Approach	Considerations and Lessons Learned
DAU has used games in several Web-based courses to help students retain factual knowledge. In one lesson, over 30 different organizational acronyms appeared. To help the students learn this new organizational language, course designers added a game called House of Acronyms at the end of the lesson. After being dealt a hand of acronyms, students must select the card that matches the description appearing on the screen. If they are correct, their winnings are increased. Wrong answers require a payment to the"House."	Students reported that they enjoyed the use of a limited number of games within the DAU courses. During course validation trials, students mentioned the need to make sure that the use of gaming interactions does not increase the time required for completing the lesson. Given the time demands in the workplace, students stressed the need to keep the lessons as efficient as possible. Again, the use of a highly graphical interface over the Internet requires that students install a plug-in and download the graphics to their computers.

Figure 8.3. Page from the House of Cards, to teach acronyms.

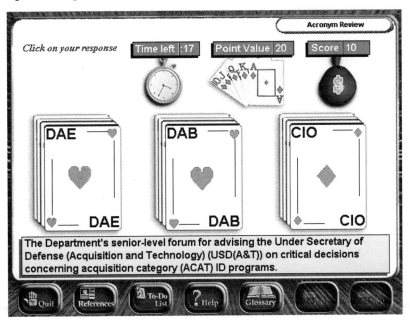

Table 8.5. DAU's approach to testing.

DAU's Web Approach	Considerations and Lessons Learned
DAU students are allowed three trials on each test. If a student fails to demonstrate mastery, the student is told to contact his or her assigned faculty member. The faculty member monitors reports to see if students have failed to reach mastery. When a student does not demonstrate mastery, the faculty member reviews the questions missed on each trial. Based on this item analysis, the faculty member develops an individualized plan for helping the student improve his or her performance. When the faculty member is satisfied that the student is ready for a retest, he or she allows access to the test on the Web. DAU students are required to complete courses as part of job certification requirements. Therefore, testing is critical. At the present time, DAU is addressing test security using the following strategies: Random generation of test items from item pools so that students get unique combinations of test items. Random placement of distractors within test items.	Effective testing over the Internet requires the use of a database. A database is used to: • store pools of items so that tests can be randomly generated for each learning objective • track the number of test attempts • report scores and item analyses to the faculty member • present recommended remediation strategies to students • retest only objectives not previously mastered • prevent the student from seeing the same item more than once • require students who are not demonstrating mastery to contact the faculty member within a set number of days. Your course management system (for testing and data collection) must be in place before you begin designing and deploying Web-based training. Without such a system, you will be unable to track student performance.

INSTRUCTIONAL METHODOLOGY: RESEARCH PROJECTS

Mandatory and optional research activities can extend students' learning beyond traditional lessons by using the vast power of the Internet. The design team's approach to recommending resources on the Web took into account the irregular quality of Web resources, students' varied experience with the Web, and students' need for feedback, as table 8.6 shows. The sample screen in figure 8.5 shows a resources page that offers students a link to the Web.

SUMMARY

The key to a successful Web-based learning environment is a comprehensive design that considers technical, instructional, and fac-

Figure 8.4. Pages from a test and a status report.

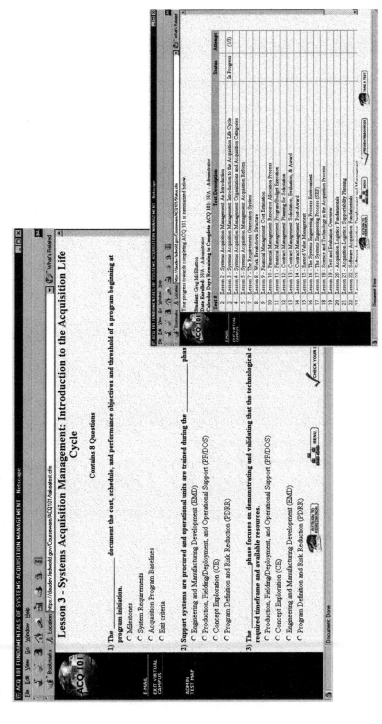

Table 8.6. DAU's approach to Web links.

DAU's Web Approach	Considerations and Lessons Learned
In validating courses, the DAU design team discovered that Web links within lessons needed to be managed carefully. Some students who were unfamiliar with the Web environment were unable to find their way back to the lesson. DAU's design solution is to offer students selected Web links after they complete the core lesson materials. The core lesson brings the student to a unique hypertext markup language (HTML) lesson exit page. After completing the core learning, the student may surf the Web. Within selected courses, students are required to complete and submit research assignments. The assignments require students to use course materials and Web links. When an assignment is complete, students submit the assignment to faculty members. Faculty members review the assignments and provide written feedback to the students.	Web-based training provides unlimited potential to introduce students to Web resources that they can use long after training has ended. Before adding a link to your course: • Screen the site to make sure that its contents are accurate and reliable. • Assess the likelihood that the site will be maintained and available in the future. Before using the technique of having students submit research assignments for grading, calculate the workload for the assigned faculty. It is critical that faculty can provide timely feedback to students. In addition, course designers should develop scoring guides and sample answers for the faculty.

Figure 8.5. A resources page that offers a link to the Web.

REVIEW RESOURCES

Lesson 3: Describing Agency Needs and Conducting Market Research

Congratulations! You have completed this lesson. Your next steps are as follows:

- Step 1: Learn How To Do Web-Based Online Market Searches
- Step 2: Visit the i-Mart Research Tool
- Step 3: Review the Lesson Summary
- Step 4: Take the Next Lesson

Step 1: Learn How To Do Web-Based Online Market Searches

Basic research skills are necessary for conducting online market research. This book ulty support requirements. It is critical to provide faculty members with training in how to instruct via the Web. DAU faculty members receive training in the following topics:

- the role of faculty members in the new environment
- the technical aspects of operating in the Web-based learning environment
- the techniques used for encouraging, monitoring, and reinforcing collaborative learning through synchronous and asynchronous communication tools
- the trends to look for when identifying students who may need additional assistance
- the most effective ways for responding to inquiries
- the uses of other communication technologies to augment Web-based delivery.

After the initial training, new DAU faculty members receive continued support using Web-based technologies.

SUGGESTED READINGS

Dillion, C., and S. Walsh. (1992). "Faculty: The Neglected Resource in Distance Education." *The American Journal of Distance Education,* 6(3), 5–21.

Gehlauf, D., M. Shatz, and T. Frye. (1991). "Faculty Perception of Interactive Instructional Strategies: Implications for Training." *The American Journal of Distance Education,* 5(3), 20–28.

Moore, M., and G. Kearsley. (1996). *Distance Education: A Systems View.* Belmont, CA: Wadsworth.

Schaeffer, J., P. Kipper, C. Farr, and D. Muscarella. (1990). "Preparing Faculty and Designing Courses for Delivery via Audio Teleconferencing." *PAEA Journal,* Spring, 11–18.

THE AUTHORS

Sharon G. Fisher is a leader in the field of instructional systems design. She has more than 23 years of experience in all facets of instructional systems design, development, delivery, and evaluation.

She has worked for Human Technology (HT) for the past 20 years. During this time, Fisher has been responsible for the design, development, and evaluation of thousands of hours of instructional materials using all types of instructional methods and media.

Fisher has made presentations at more than 12 national conferences on the use of Web-based training. She has published four books and two articles on instructional design and evaluation. She currently serves on the Instructional Systems Design Advisory Board for the U.S. Department of Agriculture Graduate School.

Will S. Peratino manages the design, development, and fielding of more than 70 distance learning courses for the Defense Acquisition University. He chairs the Content Advocacy Group of the Advanced Distributed Learning (ADL) Initiative. This initiative is sponsored by the Office of the Secretary of Defense and the White House and is looking at innovative ways to use technology to support lifelong learning.

Prior to joining the Defense Acquisition University, Peratino managed the design, development, and fielding of 48 multimedia courses for the U.S. Naval Health Sciences Education and Training Command. These courses provide hundreds of hours of just-in-time training to medical personnel worldwide

Chapter 9

Addressing Engineering Curricula: An Audiographics Case Study

Sue Faust

Distance Education Specialist
Instructional Communications Systems,
University of Wisconsin-Extension

> [A]udio teleconferencing is a very cost effective method when one balances the gains in interactivity and the relatively low cost of the technology. (Garrison, 1990, p. 18)

BACKGROUND

Imagine you'd like to offer an outreach course to engineers for professional development purposes. Or you want to satisfy the educational needs of adults returning to school because they are seeking to move from a two-year nursing degree to a four-year (RN) degree? And of course, these needs must be met in as cost-effective a manner as possible, preferably with little investment in additional equipment.

These are actual needs that Instructional Communications Systems (ICS) has responded to in its extensive teleconferencing history. ICS is a unit of the Continuing Education Division within the University of Wisconsin-Extension (UW).

This case study features the use of audiographics conferencing software for teaching an undergraduate engineering mechanics course on statics. Statics is a branch of physics that deals with the analysis of forces in structures. Students are primarily at the sophomore level, and this course partially fulfills requirements of several engineering curricula. Professor Frank Gonzales, based at the University of Wisconsin-Marathon, leads the course.

Before exploring the case study course in detail, let's examine how the audiographics technology works. Present-day audiographics systems allow for two-way visual and audio interaction. As a distance education platform, audiographics is cost-effective, flexible, synchronous, and highly interactive. Here in Wisconsin, students can take part in courses from any of 25 public locations at various University of Wisconsin campuses. ICS uses DataBeam's MeetingTools product.

As a distance education platform, audiographics is cost-effective, flexible, synchronous, and highly interactive.

All sites use 486-level personal computers and have one or more high-resolution color monitors, keyboard, a graphics tablet with stylus, document scanner, high-speed modem, and an audio teleconferencing unit with several microphones and a speaker. Two dedicated telephone lines are required. Audio communications between sites are transmitted via standard telephone lines and use an in-house conferencing service. The second telephone line, linked by a computer data bridge located at ICS, is used to share visuals with each other. As a result of these linkages, students are joined together in a virtual classroom that provides synchronous audio and collaboration between all participants.

During a class, an instructor can display graphics that were created and stored on the system prior to the class. The graphics could be handwritten formulas, line drawings, or color images, like traditional slides or overhead transparencies. A blank screen can be used for on-the-spot sketching of the answer to a participant's questions. By using a scanner, an instructor or student at any location can send a report or an article from a morning newspaper to all locations and display it for discussion.

Students at any location can introduce visuals, including high-resolution graphics, photographs, annotations, and hand-drawn sketches. Participants at each site are able to view graphics simultaneously. They may also annotate and amend visuals using a variety of drawing icons included with the software. Thus they are able to interact with the information displayed on the workbook page.

Sessions are very interactive. At any time during a teleconference, participants can use a microphone to make comments or ask questions. In addition, the bridging software at ICS allows for the creation of subconferences. That is, the class as a whole can be broken down into multiple discussion groups connected with audio capability. Thus students at opposite corners of the state can be connected to explore a discussion question. This is an invaluable feature in that it allows students at one location to interact with distant classmates with whom contact would otherwise be quite limited. This kind of interaction also contributes greatly to a sense of class cohesion.

STATICS AT UW

The students for the statics class are dispersed widely throughout the Wisconsin. Depending on their location, they meet at any number of the 25 remote sites equipped with audiographic capability. Class size has averaged between 25 and 35 students and has reached up to 50 students. These students are found at five to 10 different cities within Wisconsin.

This particular class has been taught via audiographics since the fall of 1991. Prior to that, it had been taught face-to-face since 1981, and it continues to be taught that way at larger campuses in the state. The decision to offer the class with a distance education technology was prompted by student requests for this class at various University of Wisconsin campuses, where the enrollments were too low (one to five students) for the class to be offered economically. The use of audiographics offered a way to meet the educational need by combining these small groups of students together into a single, virtual classroom.

ICS provided training support for the course development process. Gonzales was supported by the following training plan:

- training related to the use of equipment
- training related to the software features
- consultation provided in an instructional designer to discuss content and delivery strategies
- practice and rehearsal sessions
- training of site support staff that would be present at each remote site.

The development of a course for delivery with audiographics, like that of any other distance education course, brings with it challenges. The main challenge this instructor experienced centered on technical problems, which caused him to lose valuable class time. To make up that time, he increased the number of class sessions from three to four per week.

Students, like faculty, also face challenges in distance education. According to Gonzales, students need to be more responsible for their own learning in a distance education environment than in a traditional classroom. Another challenge for students in distance education is learning to work with technology. Effective use of conferencing software is essential if learners are to be active participants. Kearsley (1990) encourages faculty to develop ways to put students at ease with the equipment required for a particular distance education class as well as to provide opportunities for practice with the various features of the software.

The use of audiographics for this engineering class has proved successful for Gonzales. Including both visual and aural communication channels, this technology provides solid platforms for communication of content as well as discussion needs. And in a day when many colleges are exploring other distance education technologies, Gonzales feels the medium is appropriate for the course as well as his teaching style.

REFERENCES

Garrison, D.R. (1990). "An Analysis and Evaluation of Audio Teleconferencing to Facilitate Education at a Distance." *The American Journal of Distance Education, 4*(3), 13–24.

Kearsley, Greg. (1990). *Teacher Training for Distance Education.* Manual prepared for GW Television, George Washington University.

THE AUTHOR

Sue Faust is a distance educational specialist at Instructional Communications Systems (ICS) at the University of Wisconsin-Extension. She holds a master's degree in continuing adult and vocational education from the University of Wisconsin. She has nine years' experience developing training programs and materials for computer software products. At ICS, Faust supports the University of Wisconsin faculty in the use of audiographics teleconferencing for instructional purposes. In addition, Faust is a part-time instructor at Madison Area Technical College.

Chapter 10

Training for Interactivity: A Case Study of the Wisconsin Public Service Commission

Bruce E. Dewey

Outreach Manager and Distance Education Specialist
Instructional Communications Systems,
University of Wisconsin-Extension

Members of the Division of Water, Compliance and Consumer Affairs (DWCCA), a unit of the Public Service Commission of Wisconsin (PSC), faced the following questions when they made their first move into distance education and videoconferencing in 1996: How can we reach more than 550 municipal water utilities that have staffs ranging from three to more than 100, and how can we keep them up-to-date on information about regulations, administrative policies, and consumer affairs?

Once division members identified these needs, they reviewed their former practices. In the past, the PSC had sent a team of three or four professional staff members to three or four sites throughout the state to conduct training sessions that lasted up to four hours. The small utilities would also have to send their staff, frequently a great distance, to attend the seminar training sessions. Training was a considerable investment in the cost of travel for many staff and participants and in the time they spent away from the office, which often amounted to several hours for a session. The PSC staff could be away from the office for 40 hours or more in a year to conduct a series of six or seven seminars on a given topic.

Videoconferencing equipment became available in a PSC building that was built in the early 1990s. Although the DWCCA had used the equipment so staff could participate in hearings without having to be on site, the division hadn't used it for training. The head of the DWCCA wanted to develop a prototype training project that would focus on the participants' goals and would also be adaptable by other divisions within the PSC.

The PSC staff wanted to have one of its staff members present at each site during the training. This on-site coordinator would do the following:

- be a presence for the division at the remote sites
- oversee administrative concerns
- assist the teaching faculty with their interaction with the participants.

The teaching staff were from PSC. Training support came from the Instructional Communications Services (ICS) at the University of Wisconsin-Extension. Working with the ICS training staff, PSC staff developed a plan that involved the following:

- training of the PSC staff to teach in a videoconferencing environment
- implementing a workshop for the teaching staff before they started their development activities to discuss alternatives
- holding a practice or rehearsal session for the teaching staff
- training of the PSC staff members who would be present at each training site.

ICS and PSC conducted several of these sessions. They began the process by holding a general workshop of about 2.5 hours for the PSC teaching staff. It focused on the differences between classroom teaching and videoconferencing. The two-way audio and two-way video capability allowed staff members to see and hear their peers interact throughout the exercise. It also permitted interaction in an easy and nonthreatening way.

First, ICS gave a basic introduction to itself and videoconferencing. Depending on the number of participants, ICS staff used the camera to show the sites and conduct introductions.

> *The two-way audio and two-way video capability allowed staff members to see and hear their peers interact throughout the exercise.*

Participants then took part in an introductory activity, which appears in figure 10.1. This activity introduces participants to videoconferencing and doubles as an icebreaker. The training staff used a document camera, which operates a little like a high-tech overhead projector, to show the figure to participants at each site.

The site coordinators distributed copies of the sheet for the participants to complete. Each sheet had two column heads, one labeled traditional classroom and the other labeled videoconferencing classroom, with bulleted spaces left blank for participants to list the features of each classroom. Then the instructor introduced the activity by

Figure 10.1. Features of the traditional classroom and the videoconferencing classroom.

Traditional Classroom	Videoconferencing Classroom
• One room	•
• Everyone can see one another	•
• Design by one person	•
• Overheads and flip charts	•
• Instructor provides energy	•
• Long training segments	•

explaining that participants were to compare features of a traditional classroom with those of a videoconferencing classroom, such as:

- In the traditional classroom, there is only one room. In the videoconferencing, audiographics, or computer situation, there are two or more rooms to consider.
- In the traditional classroom, you can see everyone all of the time. In the videoconferencing, audiographics, or computer situation, you are limited in what you can see. What a participant can see varies with the type of technology. In the case of audiographics and the computer, what one can see varies with the type of software a participant has and the other sites have.

After giving the examples, the instructor asked participants to break up into small groups or to talk to one or two people close to them to explore the differences. Usually, we give them three to five minutes. Then each group reported back, and the training staff wrote what they reported on the chart or on a flipchart. The trainers then summarized what they reported and elaborated on their observations from experience.

This activity is a model. In training, we at ICS have used many variations on it, such as a focus on the following:

- protocol differences
- cognitive differences
- affective differences.

If we are doing this as a presentation, rather than over a technology network, we also have a wide number of ways in which we can divide the group. In addition, we can ask different groups to focus on different perspectives, such as instructor, student, administrator, or support personnel.

After this interactive exercise (and good icebreaker), the PSC teaching staff met to decide on the content of the sessions. They then met with the trainers and discussed the areas on which each teaching staff member would be working. The group discussed the content and the possible activities, evaluating the pros and cons as well as the logistical concerns for each activity.

For three weeks or so, members of the PSC teaching staff worked on developing their portion of the program. During this time, they were in consultation with the training staff for advice, suggestions, and comments about their activities. The next step was the rehearsal. As part of this step, we used a site-to-site approach. Several PSC staff who would be working as the distant site coordinators during the training event worked at the distant site. Immediately following the rehearsal, and the following discussion, we held a training session for the site coordinators. Finally, on the day of the training event, the ICS training staff was able to look from the videoconference bridge, which connected the sites, to see that everything went as planned. The complete process, from planning to implementation, took about eight weeks.

A team of three or four specialists, one of whom served as a moderator, led each seminar. Each one of them presented a segment of the content. The specialists used interaction, such as role play and question and answer activities, throughout and kept lecturing to a minimum. A site coordinator from the DWCAA, who had received advanced training, was present at each of the distant sites to ensure that participants had the best experience possible. The coordinator worked the equipment, handled last minute administrative duties, and helped the participants work through the activities that the specialist-instructor led.

Each seminar lasted three hours. The seminars were distributed to three or four sites at a time and repeated two or three times to provide coverage to the state. This allowed the program to be completed within a two-week period. The sites that were used included state office buildings, university classrooms, and public schools.

Participants appreciated the PSC's efforts to provide this training. The small water utilities are widely dispersed through the state. It had been prohibitively expensive for them to send staff a long distance for previous programs, so many of them were unable to attend. The cost for the PSC was cut dramatically because the seminar leaders did not have to travel but were able to present from a room within the building where they worked.

The results of the evaluations of the first seminar series indicated that the DWCCA was successful in accomplishing its objectives. There were more than 200 participants from the water utilities throughout the state. With videoconferencing, travel was cut significantly for both the presenters and the participants.

The cost ... was cut dramatically because the seminar leaders did not have to travel but were able to present from a room within the building where they worked.

In the second year, there were two different seminars. The first one dealt with rates and accounting issues, and the second with consumer issues. Nearly 500 municipal water utility staff members participated in this series.

The DWCCA has deemed this project a success and continues to use videoconferencing for two sessions a year, one in the spring and one in the fall.

SUMMARY

The value of knowing how a process or an idea was implemented is that it can help others recreate and reposition it for their own needs. As trainers, we face challenges everywhere, including the constraints of time and financial and other resources. We can learn from the mistakes of others (that information is often invaluable) and try to ensure that our designs and applications don't fall into the same traps. Every trainer that works with learning technologies will have a story to tell about working with the learners, about how well the interaction worked (or didn't work), and if the activities contributed to the learning process.

The authors of the case studies in chapters 8, 9, and 10 hope that you, the reader, can take one idea or concept from this study and apply it to your own situation. Open sharing of experiences and lessons learned will help all of us in our goal to achieve success as a 21st-century trainer. One idea can change the way you think, react, or help support your success.

THE AUTHOR

Bruce E. Dewey is an outreach manager, and distance education specialist at Instructional Communications Systems (ICS) at the University of Wisconsin-Extension. He holds a master's degree from Syracuse University and has completed postmaster's work in instructional technology, instructional development, and continuing education. He has taught at the University of Wisconsin-Extension for 23 years and has worked with many instructional design workshops.

Section 4:

A Guide to Real-World Application

Chapter 11

Bringing It All Together

INTRODUCTION

One of the greatest challenges learners—including trainers—face in applying newly acquired information and knowledge is doing so with ease. In this section, I would like to provide recommendations in the form of a guide to support you through the process of taking classroom exercises and adapting them to a distance learning situation.

The preceding sections provided the foundation and content for creating interactive distance learning exercises that really work. This section is designed to help you apply those principles. It is not intended to be a one-size-fits-all solution to adapting your exercises, but a visual and mental guide to help you think about the important aspects of your distance learning courses, target audience, learning objectives, media selection, and desired participation outcomes.

Time management is often a juggling act. I was a participant in a recent meeting at which managers were talking about doing three versions of a course via distance learning. One abbreviated version with the key points would last about an hour; another would be a daylong course covering all the significant learning areas; and the third version would be an extensive seminar and learning resource opportunity to train someone from start to finish.

I thought about that meeting as I was writing this section, and I wanted to be sure that I provided you with the important points discussed in the book. This is not intended to be microwave training— quick but missing the subtleties. It is intended to provide you with key areas to think about as you successfully adapt your exercises to help the learners enjoy their distance learning experience and really learn by participation.

GETTING STARTED

The process begins by selecting the audience you want to reach and the exercises you want to teach. Following are some of the key steps in the process:

- Identify the target audience and one or more locations.
- Select the course you want to adapt and review existing interactive exercises.
- Analyze feedback from the learners and instructors for effectiveness.
- Identify all instructional methods used (for example, games, role play, group discussion).
- Identify all presentation methods used (for example, video, CBT, print).

UNDERSTAND THE DIFFERENCES BETWEEN ON-SITE INTERACTIVITY AND DISTANCE LEARNING

As you plan your distance learning activities, carefully think about the ways learners perceive the differences between on-site interactivity and distance learning. Following are some important differences:

- not being in the same physical location as the trainer
- not having the opportunity to network with peers for collaboration

144

- having to use technology to complete the learning-inter-activity process
- often being unsure about how to interact
- not being sure what the trainer expects
- not knowing how to ask questions (or appearing stupid "in front" of many people)
- being unsure about how to clarify learning content.

Trainers have many of the same concerns. Others include:

- having peers see and hear their instructional delivery
- not knowing how to use appropriate technologies for inter-activity
- not knowing how to foster interactivity at remote sites and from one remote site to another
- not wanting to appear less than skilled and professional in the use of technologies.

FOCUS ON THE LEARNER

Because of these differences in perception, you'll want to do the following:

- Understand the learner.
- Ensure that exercise instructions are clear and easy for learners to understand.
- Make sure learners understand their role or roles in completing the exercise.
- Provide learners with written and oral instructions on how to use the equipment.
- Review what the instructor expects of participants.
- Review with learners how they can apply the lessons learned to their jobs.
- Design the exercises to be both enjoyable and beneficial to the learner.
- Tell learners how get help for any questions or any support they need.

PREPARE INSTRUCTORS FOR THE NEW INTERACTIVE EXPERIENCE

The following three guiding principles will help you when you are going to train the trainer:

- Reach them with their love to instruct.
- Provide a means for voicing issues and concerns.
- Instruct via the technology so new instructors experience the experience.

Distance learning instructors can be most effective if they do the following:

- Know the environment.
- Work as a team player.
- Create instructor support tools and procedures.
- Integrate support with all team members.
- Monitor programs, course materials, and learners' feedback for quality.

Because you must find ways to connect with learners you may never see face-to-face, be sure to develop formats and strategies for interactive exercises and create the following:

- a mixture of different types of exercises to retain learners' interest
- interactive exercises that are personalized
- interactive activities, visuals, and print materials
- learner support tools and procedures.

Ask yourself key questions to help adapt your exercises for distance learning:

- Can the learners complete the exercises on their own without a trainer or facilitator?
- Will the learners:

  —need any specific guidance as they go along?

—need to see a visual or reference material in order to complete the exercise?

—need to collaborate with team members or other learners?

—have a way to ask questions during the learning experience?

—be tested along the way or at the end of an exercise?

—receive feedback on their answers as they complete the exercises?

—know how to apply the learning content to their own jobs?

FACTORS INFLUENCING MEDIA SELECTION

The learning technologies you choose will depend on a variety of factors including the exercises you will convert and the hardware and software available to you. Make all media selection decisions based on fact—what would be logical to meet learning objectives and equipment available at learner sites—not emotion—a bias toward one method or another. Before you decide, do the following:

- Ensure that your course tasks, objectives, and requirements are clearly defined.
- Be sure you understand the following distance learning technologies:

  —Teletraining is synchronous two-way audio and one-way video instruction conducted with groups of learners. The learners can see and hear the instructor, but the instructor can only hear the learners, and learners can only hear one another.

  —Video teleconferencing is synchronous, two-way audio and two-way video instruction conducted with groups of learners. Learners can see and hear the instructor, the instructor can see and hear the learners, and learners can see and hear one another.

  —Audio conferencing can be audio teletraining (two-way synchronous audio-only instruction) or audiographics (two-way synchronous audio with computer graphics sent to each participant's computer).

—CD-ROM is asynchronous, self-paced, interactive instruction conducted on a multimedia computer. Although a number of learners may be working on the same lesson, each learner is usually expected to work alone and at his or her own pace.

—Internet or intranet instruction takes a variety of forms. It may be either synchronous (similar to video conferencing) or asynchronous (similar to CD-ROM or online text-based courses).

- Review all hardware and software capabilities at the learners' and the origination sites.
- Examine the current exercises or identify new exercise components that ask the learners to:

—demonstrate

—explain

—listen

—tell what they have learned

—work with other team members or learners

—interact with the instructor.

- Identify which learning technologies and distance learning methods would be best suited to help the learners successfully complete the exercise.
- Prepare a media selection analysis using a media selection instrument.
- Make a list of the different types of exercises and activities that will be used to support the learning objectives, including:

—role playing

—lecture

—games

—expert panel

—practical exercise

—team collaboration

—readings

—simulations.

- List each learning exercise or activity as synchronous (learners completing it at the same time) or asynchronous (learners completing it at a different time).

ADAPTING INSTRUCTIONAL EXERCISES TO LEARNING TECHNOLOGIES

The following lists review ways to adapt some on-site exercises and activities to various learning technologies. They provide key points for you to think about as you look at the possibilities for adapting your own exercises.

ROLE PLAYING

Role-playing exercises provide learners with opportunities to practice applying recently learned information and procedures. Following are ways to adapt role playing for different technologies:

Teletraining (satellite)

- Use visual props for effect.
- Use document camera to view objects for discussion.
- For interactivity, use telephone call-in, fax, student response systems, or computer-based input, based on equipment availability.
- Give learners turns at remote sites and create exercises to allow remote sites to evaluate the effectiveness of each group.

Video Teleconferencing

- Ensure that only one learner speaks at a time. This is especially important in this method of delivery because one voice can eliminate the other, and silence will be the end result. Two people speaking at the same time will void the input!

Audio Conferencing

- Select a narrator or instructor to set the stage for the role play and stop at integral learning points, if helpful for the learning objectives.
- Let learners take an individual or team approach to verbalize the role play situation.
- Have remote site learners participate after the role play by a round robin activity to provide feedback or analysis.

CD-ROM

- Make sure the "Welcome" screen clearly reflects what to do and how to do it.
- Design the exercises to show which types of choices are available to the learners (do they have to go in a specific sequence, for example).
- Create a video scenario at critical points in the exercise that include audio and video response choices about what should be done next in the role play.
- Design a feedback response system with branching and remedial training, as needed, based on the user's response.

Internet or Intranet

- Create asynchronous role-play scenarios like those recommended for CD-ROM.
- Create synchronous adaptations similar to the video teleconferencing examples (with the exception that the learner would normally be alone at a computer, not in a group setting).

LECTURE

Lectures are to communicate information and ideas to the learners, and good lectures feel like a spontaneous conversation between the instructor and learners. In the resident classroom example, the instructor can maintain interest by:

- using a conversational tone
- incorporating stories to illustrate points
- maintaining eye contact with learners
- telling the learners what you are going to tell them
- giving them the detail of the information
- summarizing by telling the learners what you told them
- providing feedback opportunities for the learners.

In converting activities to distance learning, instructors can do everything but keep eye contact with the learners. Learning technologies enable instructors to spot "electronic body language" through the use of interactive learner keypads, randomly calling on learners at different remote sites, seeing them in a two-way video environment, receiving fax or email responses, and having the availability of a toll free call-in line.

Following are some ideas for converting your lectures into distance learning exercises and activities:

Teletraining and Video Teleconferencing

- Develop graphics suited to the project to fit the TV screen.
- Use colors for the background and text that ensure ease of viewing.
- Review good principles and practices that apply to converting visuals (in using colors, font sizes, artwork).
- Change camera angles on the instructor to keep learners interested.
- Call on different remote site learners to stimulate participation.
- Select videos that support the learning objectives and show in short (10-minute or less) time segments.

- Discuss videos with remote site learners to stimulate thinking and remote site collaboration.

CD-ROM

- Keep the lecture short, concise, and to the point.
- Develop exercises to ensure learners understand the key points.
- Use a narrator that moves the lecture along and show pictures or graphics as the lecture moves along.
- Include review questions after each main point and a feedback system for the learner.
- Design practical exercises and simulations to have learners demonstrate mastery of the lesson or learning module.

Internet or Intranet

- Speed up running of the program by having learners download the lesson on their hard drives.
- Design exercises that can be done in asynchronous or synchronous formats. Both ways can be used effectively.
- Use these and the video teleconference recommendations if a synchronous format is selected.
- Include learner quizzes or activities at the end of the lecture with specific links to mastery of the lecture content and practical, on-the-job applications.

GAMES

Games are to reinforce and review learning content by allowing learners to apply what they have learned and have fun along the way! Enjoyment of the distance learning experience is important to learners' overall satisfaction of the event.

Popular classroom games include those based on the TV show *Jeopardy.* You can group remote site learners into teams, by organizational area, or in any other way that would stimulate collaboration. If possible, offer some inexpensive prizes that can be given out at remote sites for participation and winning (answering the right question) as well as for the team that scores the highest amount of points with correct answers.

Teletraining

- Use either an electronic format (electronic computer images projected on the TV monitor) or the document camera to project the game board.
- Choose a host or use the instructor to conduct the game.
- Call on teams at remote sites.
- Pose the subject category questions among the remote sites in a round-robin process.
- Keep a scoreboard in back of you to show the teams with correct answers.
- Review all key subject categories at the end of the game.
- Ensure that learners have time to ask questions or send them by fax or electronic delivery.

Video Teleconference

- Follow above recommendations for teletraining.
- Provide clear directions that only one person can speak at a time when called upon.
- Take care to control learners' responses because this type of method is voice activated.
- Rotate the originating locations to show the site teams that are responding to the question.

Audio Conferencing and Audiographics

- Distribute a paper copy of the game board with categories and point values in the support packet of information each learner received before the event.

- Have each learner participate individually (instead of in a team approach) as the learners will most likely be at individual workstations.
- If there are a large number of learners, assign each one to a predesignated team (use a team name that fits their work environment).
- Tell learners to mark off categories and questions after they are answered.
- With audiographics, send the computer image of the game board. As questions are answered, send an updated image to the learners.

CD-ROM

- State all directions simply and clearly.
- Explain what to do if the learner does not know the answer to one or more questions.
- For incorrect answers, provide remedial branching to show the correct answer (and why).
- Provide a performance review at the end of the game with the number and percentage of correct answers.

Internet or Intranet

- Conduct the game in an asynchronous format similar to that in the CD-ROM example.
- Speed up the game by telling learners to download it on their hard drives.
- Add hyperlink remedial branching to show correct answers and why and add links to appropriate additional readings or reference materials on that subject.

EXPERT PANEL

Expert panels provide learners with the opportunity to ask specific questions to a diverse group of leaders in any given area. They may be physically located at the same origination site or geographically dispersed.

Teletraining, Video Teleconferencing, and Audio Teleconference

- Establish protocol procedures for how learners can interact with the experts.
- Moderate the event and control the number and length of panelists' interactions with learners.
- Instructors should solicit questions from different sites and learners by use of student response pads, a toll-free number, a fax line, or email for learners' interactions with panelists.
- Use audio and show a picture of the panel member with your document camera (audio conferencing method excluded) if he or she can't go to origination site.
- Summarize the key learning points at the end of the panel discussion.

CD-ROM

- Develop video clips of experts giving their thoughts on specific topics.
- Provide the learner with a menu of these topics for random selection.
- Develop situational scenarios where the learner selects a certain answer to a problem-solving question, and based on the response, the expert panel member can comment on the selected answer.

Internet or Intranet

- Follow the recommendations for CD-ROM if the exercise is to be conducted in an asynchronous manner.
- Follow the recommendations for video teleconferencing if the exercise is done in a synchronous manner.

- Set up a chat room for learner interaction.
- Establish email connectivity for the learners to reach expert panel members. (Provide specific guidance as to the type of questions, frequency, and availability to learners of this type of interaction.)

PRACTICAL EXERCISE

Practical exercises provide students with the opportunity to apply what they have learned to a given situation or a series of situations.

Teletraining

- Practical application exercises can require an audio, visual, or combined response by the learners.
- Instruct teams at remote sites to send a visual response by fax or email.
- Select any excellent visual responses as discussion points for key learning.
- Show each visual to all sites by placing it on the document camera.
- Instruct learners to call a toll-free number to discuss a key point on the air or to notify the instructor for postevent feedback.

Video Teleconference

- Use methods utilized for on-site or resident classrooms where the instructor and the learners can interact with both audio and video capabilities.
- Select one or more learners at remote sites to show their application with either a video (using the document camera or PC) or audio demonstration.
- Ask one or more sites to collaborate on preparing a demonstration (to vary the type of responses and increase the number of interactive participants).

- Let one person describe what was done, one person demonstrate, and one person summarize the practical application.
- Ask one or more of the remote site learners to give their input or pose any question regarding a demonstration.

Audio Conferencing

- Distribute necessary exercise support materials in the packet of information sent to remote site learners before the event. Details must be clearly spelled out with necessary graphics to ensure that learners know exactly what to do and how to do it.
- Instruct learners to send by fax or email any exercise that instructors should check visually.
- Allow learners to send a visual as a pretest, during the event, or as a posttest within two hours of the event.
- Summarize the key learning points of any exercise or learning module or ask a volunteer to do so.

Audiographics

- Show a correct solution or examples on the computer screen for all to see in a synchronous manner.
- Draw to annotate key areas, show deficiencies, and add additional illustrations to summarize key learning points.

Internet or Intranet

- Refer to the recommendations for CD-ROM if the exercise is to be conducted in an asynchronous manner.
- Show learners both the "wrong" and "right" way to complete the exercise.
- Instruct learners to correct the wrong way.
- Provide feedback branches to congratulate the learners for all correct answers.

- Provide remedial branches for any wrong answers given.
- Use both audio and video feedback.
- Follow recommendations for video teleconferencing technology for exercises conducted in a synchronous manner.

TEAM COLLABORATION

Team collaboration is to have groups of learners work on a specific exercise or a series of exercises to accomplish a specific learning outcome. The team may be disbanded after one exercise or stay together for an entire course or learning module.

Teletraining

- Advise teams to select a team leader, a team spokesperson, and a team member to summarize their findings (the more participants for each interaction will increase the team stimulation).
- Let teams collaborate before the event, during an event, and after as a remote site exercise.
- Choose various types of media to set the stage and support the audio instructions, such as videos, objects under the document camera, email attachments, and fax.

Video Teleconference

- Observe the team collaboration process.
- Ask learners to give their feedback on any team input.
- Ask remote site team leaders to present supporting presentations by their team.
- Open the discussions up using a round-robin process by remote sites.
- Invite teams to use one or more visual examples to support their findings.
- Get summary comments from a remote team member.
- Present summary as well to ensure learners' understanding of key learning points and practical applications.

Audio Conferencing and Audiographics

- Assign teams by remote location with selected team members assigned to different roles, such as a team leader, team spokesperson, and team member to summarize key points and findings.
- Use visuals on the computer screen if audiographic capabilities are being used to support a team, present a challenge to a team, or summarize key findings to the entire group of learners.
- Ask learners to comment on other team findings, if they are operating in an asynchronous fashion at their remote site.
- Invite learners to provide a summary for a particular team, if they are operating in an asynchronous fashion at their remote site.

CD-ROM

- Prepare preprogrammed responses by a narrator (audio and video) to any team scenario.
- Provide a fact sheet for the problem, opportunity, or challenge that the preprogrammed team will address.
- Offer choices and branching for learners' responses to explain why an answer is correct or offer remedial information for any incorrect answer.
- Ensure that a team collaboration is necessary for this learning module, as this method of delivery is not the ideal technology for this type of exercise.

Internet or Intranet

- Refer to the advice for CD-ROM delivery if learners are in an asynchronous mode.
- Establish teams in different locations if learners are in a synchronous mode. You can establish teams in advance and

team members can work on an exercise before the synchronous event.

- Assign team members specific online research and have them report findings to their team members.
- Define specific roles for team members to cover all the key learning points.
- Get team members to summarize their team's findings in the synchronous learning event and post them on a specific Website.
- Summarize the key learning points for the course.
- Instruct learners to read the team findings on a designated site and ask questions or provide feedback.

READING

Reading exercises can provide background material, basic reading essential to a course or learning module, and additional knowledge for those learners wishing to delve further into any particular subject area.

Teletraining

- Assign specific reading assignments, tied to specific course modules, before the live event, and let the learners know that you will call on them for their input and feedback during the live event.
- Call on different sites to encourage participation for as many remote learners as possible.
- Discuss a specific section of the reading assignment and randomly call on sites or learners for their analysis or opinions.
- Use the readings as a remote site discussion prior to the live event (and as postevent discussions for practical applications to the learners' job).

Video Teleconference

- Choose learners to analyze, discuss, support, or defend the readings.

- Go to as many sites as possible where learners can be seen and heard. Plan which sites will be asked for any specific dialogue.
- Let each site discuss how to use the specific readings to strengthen their knowledge base for practical, on-the-job applications.

Audio Conferencing

- Assign readings before the event to help the learners gain comprehension of the topic of the audio conference.
- Assign readings that show real-world applications of the basic learning points.
- Ask each learner to write down any questions on the reading assignment to ask during a question-and-answer segment or where appropriate during the live session.
- Assign extra credit advanced readings for those who want to volunteer to discuss them and their relevance to the discussions.

CD-ROM and Internet or Intranet

- Assign readings based on major learning modules or content.
- Develop CD-ROM to position readings subsequent to description of learning content.
- Create exercises to help the learners reinforce the key learning points and coordinate with assigned reading.
- Integrate any appropriate video clips to reinforce and demonstrate the key points in content and readings.
- Provide an exercise to allow the learners to apply the learning concepts derived from the readings.
- Create branching to let the learner know how he or she did with the exercise.
- Create remedial branching to help learners understand why an answer was incorrect and provide a pathway for understanding the correct answer.

- Instruct students to download the exercises to their computer to speed up the running of the program if the exercises are delivered via the Internet or intranet.
- Facilitate or moderate all discussions and carefully manage the participation of all learners.

SIMULATIONS

The use of simulations is an enabling technology to allow organizations to take risk-free risks, discover engineering end results, and allow learners to apply what they have learned in a real-world environment. The learners can experience the consequences of their actions and decisions in a positive or negative fashion. Learning by using simulations most closely resembles use of the applications on the job.

Teletraining

- Develop and use simulations at the live origination site.
- Create videotapes showing simulations and show them at specific learning points.
- Instruct learners how to interact by using an interactive learner response pad, a telephone, the fax machine, and email.

Video Teleconference

- Take advantage of two-way video technology by preassigning remote site simulation exercises to be conducted by the learners.
- Do a simulation at the origination site and get learners to give their feedback, opinions, and recommendations by site.
- Equip remote locations with a simulation environment showing certain items, props, or materials that would add to the realism of the exercise.
- Show a simulation by video and randomly call on remote site learners to provide their feedback or answer questions.

Audio Conferencing and Audiographics

- Describe a situation and have others at the origination site act out the simulated situation.
- With audio only, ask learners a series of questions to test their level of knowledge as to what was right and what was wrong. (This method is not as effective as simulations with video capability.)
- With audiographics, add a graphic simulation on the computer and show the image at the remote site PCs.
- Request learners' feedback or randomly call on them to answer questions.
- Summarize key learning points after each simulation, especially where there is no video component to the exercise.

CD-ROM

- Develop and design a series of video simulations that provide for learners' feedback after each key learning point.
- Provide the learner with several options to select what went "right" and what went "wrong."
- Provide positive feedback on all right answers and remedial branching for wrong answers detailing the correct answer and why.

Internet or Intranet

- Use the recommendations for CD-ROM in an asynchronous mode.
- Use the recommendations for video teleconferencing for a synchronous mode.
- Add links to reference material or additional readings or video-based discussions focused on the key learning points of that exercise.
- Provide chat rooms or bulletin boards where learners can provide feedback and offer comments for discussion.

- Ask learners to complete an exercise to justify their decisions based on the simulated event and send it via email.
- Give feedback to learners no later than two weeks after event. The sooner the response time, the better it will be for the learners.

REVIEW OF SOUND PRINCIPLES

The following sound principles relate to any and all exercises, no matter what the distribution method might be: on site, satellite, video teleconferencing, computer-based training, audio, audiographics, and print.

- Ensure that all learners know how to use the equipment.
- Ensure that each exercise is clearly written with step-by-step instructions.
- Advise the learners exactly what is expected for each exercise.
- Explain how the learners will be participating with the instructor or other learners and what is expected of them.
- Advise that this is an active not passive learning event.
- Ensure that the learners understand how the exercise is tied to the learning objectives and how this will help them with practical on-the-job applications.
- Clearly summarize, at the end of each exercise or activity, what has been learned.
- Develop a quiz or practical exercise that shows mastery of the lesson and understanding of practical, on-the-job application.
- Develop feedback sessions for the learners.

JUST THE BEGINNING

Now that you have had an introduction to the key areas in the transition to distance learning, you're ready to further develop your distance learning expertise in interactivity exercises. The resources section at the end of the book is a guide to a menu of distance learning resources available through a variety of multiple media, such as books and Web-based information.

There are new books that are very specific, such as *The ASTD Media Selection Tool for Workplace Learning,* which provides excellent in-depth coverage of this topic. You might also be interested in developing 21st-century trainer competencies, information on which can be found in *ASTD Models for Learning Technologies.* The section also lists Websites, like http://www.blackboard.com, which will enable you to convert a course to Web-based delivery—for free!

There is a wealth of information available through many resources, and the key is to focus on what you need, to strengthen your role as a trainer who is skilled in using learning technologies. Our continuous learning, as trainers, will keep us in sync not only with the current technologies, but also with the ones that haven't surfaced yet. When they do, we'll be ready to meet them head on.

A Final Word

Effectively engaging the learners through enjoyable and technology-sensitive interactive exercises will help them succeed in the 21st century. The exercises you create can help make the difference between a ho-hum learning experience and the acquisition and application of knowledge for skill proficiency.

Exercises don't have to fit in the standard box anymore, because there is no box. You can create a hybrid approach to creating segments of exercises delivered by multiple media. Your creativity and knowledge of the learning technologies will help you design in ways never thought of before. Now, it is possible to think about the impossible and make it happen.

Think about the impact you can make by truly understanding the needs of the 21st-century learner, the new ways of learning, and the technologies that will help deliver your learning content. The interactive opportunities can help create a learning environment that will motivate your learners to increase their skill portfolio and stimulate them to aspire to lifelong learning.

When that happens, everyone wins.

Glossary of
Distance Education Terminology

WHY A GLOSSARY?

As distance education becomes more prominent on the university campus, more and more instructors and students are becoming involved in both the technical and educational aspects of distance education. It is important to understand distance education related terminology if the instruction and delivery is to be understood by all persons involved.

THE GLOSSARY

Analog: A signal that is received in the same form in which it is transmitted, while the amplitude and frequency may vary.

Amplitude: The amount of variety in a signal. Commonly thought of as the height of a wave.

American Standard Code for Information Interexchange (ASCII): A computer language used to convert letters, numbers, and control codes into a digital code understood by most computers.

Asynchronous: Communication in which interaction between parties does not take place simultaneously.

Asynchronous Transmission Mode (ATM): A method of sending data in irregular time intervals using a code such as ASCII. ATM allows most modern computers to communicate with one another easily.

Audio Bridge: A device used in audioconferencing that connects multiple telephone lines.

Audioconferencing: Voice only connection of more than two sites using standard telephone lines.

Backbone: A primary communication path connecting multiple users.

Band: A range of frequencies between defined upper and lower limits.

Bandwidth: Information carrying capacity of a communication channel.

Binary: A computer language developed with only two letters in its alphabet.

Bit: Abbreviation for a single binary digit.

Byte: A single computer word, generally eight bits.

Browser: Software that allows you to find and see information on the Internet.

Central Processing Unit (CPU): The component of a computer in which data processing takes place.

Channel: The smallest subdivision of a circuit, usually with a path in only one direction.

Codec (COder/DECoder): Device used to convert analog signals to digital signals for transmission and reconvert signals upon reception at the remote site while allowing for the signal to be compressed for less expensive transmission.

Compressed Video: When video signals are downsized to allow travel along a smaller carrier.

Compression: Reducing the amount of visual information sent in a signal by only transmitting changes in action.

Computer Assisted Instruction (CAI): Teaching process in which a computer is utilized to enhance the learning environment by assisting students in gaining mastery over a specific skill.

Cyberspace: The nebulous "place" where humans interact over computer networks. Coined by William Gibson in Neuromancer.

Desktop Videoconferencing: Videoconferencing on a personal computer.

Dial-Up Teleconference: Using public telephone lines for communications links among various locations.

Digital: An electrical signal that varies in discrete steps in voltage, frequency, amplitude, locations, etc. Digital signals can be transmitted faster and more accurately than analog signals.

Digital Video Interactive (DVI): A format for recording digital video onto compact disc allowing for compression and full motion video.

Distance Education: The process of providing instruction when students and instructors are separated by physical distance and technology, often in tandem with face-to-face communication, is used to bridge the gap.

Distance Learning: The desired outcome of distance education.

Download: Using the network to transfer files from one computer to another.

Echo Cancellation: The process of eliminating the acoustic echo in a videoconferencing room.

Electronic Mail (email): Sending messages from one computer user to another.

Facsimile (FAX): System used to transmit textual or graphical images over standard telephone lines.

Fiber Optic Cable: Glass fiber that is used for laser transmission of video, audio, and/or data.

File Transfer Protocol (FTP): A protocol that allows you to move files from a distant computer to a local computer using a network like the Internet.

Frequency: The space between waves in a signal. The amount of time between waves passing a stationary point.

Frequently Asked Questions (FAQ): A collection of information on the basics of any given subject, often used on the World Wide Web.

Full Motion Video: Signal which allows transmission of complete action taking place at the origination site.

Fully Interactive Video (two way interactive video): Two sites interact with audio and video as if they were co-located.

Home Page: A document with an address (URL) on the World Wide Web maintained by a person or organization, which contains pointers to other pieces of information.

Host: A network computer that can receive information from other computers.

Hyper Text Markup Language (HTML): The code used to create a home page and to access documents over the Web.

Hypertext Transfer Protocol (http): The protocol used to signify an Internet site is a World Wide Web (WWW) site (that is, http is a WWW address).

Hypertext: A document which has been marked up to allow a user to select words or pictures within the document, click on them, and connect to further information.

Instructional Television Fixed Service (ITFS): Microwave-based, high-frequency television used in educational program delivery.

Integrated Services Digital Network (ISDN): A telecommunications standard allowing communications channels to carry voice, video, and data simultaneously.

Interactive Media: Frequency assignment that allows for a two-way interaction or exchange of information.

Internet: An international network of networks primarily used to connect education and research networks begun by the United States government.

Internet Protocol (IP): The international standard for addressing and sending data via the Internet.

Listserv: An e-mail program that allows multiple computer users to connect onto a single system, creating an on-line discussion.

Local Area Network (LAN): Two or more local computers that are physically connected.

Microwave: Electromagnetic waves that travel in a straight line and are used to and from satellites and for short distances (i.e., up to 30 miles).

Modem: A piece of equipment to allow computers to interact with each other via telephone lines by converting digital signals to analog for transmission along analog lines.

Mosaic: An example of browser software that allows WWW use.

Multimedia: Any document which uses multiple forms of communication, such as text, audio, and/or video.

Multi-Point Control Unit (MCU): Computerized switching system which allows point-to-multipoint videoconferencing.

Netscape: An example of browser software that allows you to design a home page and to browse links on the WWW.

Network: A series of points connected by communication channels in different locations.

On-Line: Active and prepared for operation. Also suggests access to a computer network.

Origination Site: The location from which a teleconference originates.

Point of Presence (POP): Point of connection between an interexchange carrier and a local carrier to pass communications into the network.

Point-to-Point: Transmission between two locations.

Point-to-Multipoint: Transmission between multiple locations using a bridge.

PPP: A software package which allows a user to have a direct connection to the Internet over a telephone line.

Protocol: A formal set of standards, rules, or formats for exchanging data that assures uniformity between computers and applications.

Satellite TV: Video and audio signals are relayed via a communication device that orbits around the earth.

Serial Line Internet Protocol (SLIP): Allows a user to connect to the Internet directly over a high-speed modem.

Server: A computer with a special service function on a network, generally receiving and connecting incoming information traffic.

Slow Scan Converter: Transmitter/receiver of still video over narrow band channels. In real time, camera subjects must remain still for highest resolution.

Synchronous: Communication in which interaction between participants is simultaneous.

T-1 (DS-1): High speed digital data channel that is a high volume carrier of voice and/or data. Often used for compressed video teleconferencing. T-1 has 24 voice channels.

T-3 (DS-3): A digital channel which communicates at a significantly faster rate than T-1.

Telecommunication: The science of information transport using wire, radio, optical, or electromagnetic channels to transmit and receive signals for voice or data communications using electrical means.

Teleconferencing: Two way electronic communication between two or more groups in separate locations via audio, video, and/or computer systems.

Transmission Control Protocol (TCP): A protocol which makes sure that packets of data are shipped and received in the intended order.

Transponder: Satellite transmitter and receiver that receives and amplifies a signal prior to re-transmission to an earth station.

Video Teleconferencing: A teleconference including two-way video.

Uniform Resource Locator (URL): The address of a homepage on the WWW.

Uplink: The communication link from the transmitting earth station to the satellite.

World Wide Web (WWW): A graphical hypertext-based Internet tool that provides access to homepages created by individuals, businesses, and other organizations.

NOTE

The following resources were reviewed and consulted in the preparation of this publication:

Glossary. http://152.30.11.86/DEER/Houghton/Committees/distancelearn/GlossaryDistEd.html
Glossary of Terms. http://www.ctcnet.com/tips/glossary.htm
Reed, J. (1996). Videoconferencing for learning glossary. http://www.kn.pacbell.com/wired/vidconf/glossary.html
The EdWeb Dictionary. http://k12.cnidr.org:90/dic.html
Willis, B. (Ed.) (1994). Distance education: Strategies and tools. Educational Technology Publications, Inc.: Englewood Cliffs, N. J.

FOR FURTHER INFORMATION

This guide is one in a series developed by Barry Willis and the University of Idaho Engineering Outreach staff highlighting information detailed in Dr. Willis's books, *Distance Education—Strategies and Tools* and *Distance Education—A Practical Guide.* Other guides in this series include: *#1 Distance Education: An Overview, #2 Strategies for Teaching at a Distance, #3 Instructional Development for Distance Education, #4 Evaluation for Distance Educators, #5 Instructional Television, #6 Instructional Audio, #7 Computers in Distance Education, #8 Print in Distance Education, #9 Strategies for Learning at a Distance, #10 Distance Education: Research, #11 Interactive Videoconferencing in Distance Education, #12 Distance Education and the WWW,* and *#13 Copyright and Distance Education.*

Source: Distance Education at a Glance, Guide #14, by Barry Willis, Associate Dean for Outreach, University of Idaho, College of Engineering. Available on the Web at http://www.uidaho.edu/evo/distglan.html. Reprinted by permission.

Resources

This section includes books, articles, periodicals, and Websites on distance learning.

INTERACTIVE DISTANCE LEARNING BOOKS AND ARTICLES

Abernathy, Donna. (1997, December). "A Start-Up Guide to Distance Learning." *Training & Development, 51*(12), 39–47.

Auerbach, Sarah. (1999, June). "How to Shop for a Virtual Classroom." *Inside Technology Training, 3*(6), 46–52.

Barron, Tom. (1999, May-June). "Desktop IDL: Ready for Prime Time?" *Technical Training, 10*(3), 22–24.

Barron, Tom. (1999, May-June). "IDL Options Broaden for Training Providers." *Technical Training, 10*(3), 18–21.

Bernstein, Mark. (1998, May). "The Virtual Classroom: A Promising Solution for Teaching Technology." *HRMagazine, 43*(6), 30–33.

Berriman, Chris D. (1999, January-February). "A View of Networked Distance Learning from Cisco." *Multimedia & Internet Training Newsletter, 6*(1-2), 14–21.

Bersani, Mark. (1999, May-June). "A Revolution in Sales Training." *Technical Training, 10*(3), 25–27.

Biner, Paul M., et al. (1997). "The Impact of Remote-Site Group Size on Student Satisfaction and Relative Performance in Interactive Telecourses." *American Journal of Distance Education, 11*(1), 23–33.

Bischoff, Whitney Rogers, et al. (1996). "Transactional Distance and Interactive Television in the Distance Education of Health Professionals." *American Journal of Distance Education, 10*(3), 4–19.

Black, Debra. (1998, September). "Live and Online: A WBT Primer." *Training & Development, 52*(9), 34–36.

Burgess, Rick, and Margaret Driscoll. (1998, May). "How to Add Interactivity to Live, Instructor-Led International Web-Based Training." *Multimedia & Internet Training Newsletter, 5*(5), 6–8.

Campbell, J. Olin, Jane Graham, and Don McCain. (1996 Summer). "Interactive Distance Learning and Job Support Strategies for Soft Skills. *Journal of Interactive Instruction Development, 9*(1), 19–21.

Cheney, Scott, and Lisa L. Jarrett, editors. (1997). "Iowa Mold Builder Apprenticeship Program." In *Excellence in Practice, Volume 1,* (pp. 25–29). Alexandria, VA: American Society for Training & Development.

Dede, Chris. (1996). "The Evolution of Distance Education: Emerging Technologies and Distributed Learning." *American Journal of Distance Education, 10*(2), 4–36.

Dickenson, Sabrina, et al. (1998, January). "How to Build Cooperation Into CBT." *Multimedia & Internet Training Newsletter, 5*(1), 6–7.

Driscoll, Margaret. (1997, November-December). "Collaborative Learning Strategies for WBT." *Technical Training, 8*(8), 20–25.

Driscoll, Margaret. (1997, April). "Defining Internet-Based and Web-Based Training." *Performance Improvement, 36*(4), 5–9.

Eastmond, Daniel V. (1998, Summer). "Adult Learners and Internet-Based Distance Education." *New Directions for Adult and Continuing Education, 78,* 33–41.

El-Tigi, Manal, and Robert Maribe Branch. (1997, May-June). "Designing for Interaction, Learner Control, and Feedback During Web-Based Learning." *Educational Technology, 37*(3), 23–29.

"Filling the Dealer Training Pipeline at Ford." (1997, October). *Training, 34*(10), A26–30.

Fleischman, John. (1996 September-October). "The Web: New Venue for Adult Education." *Adult Learning, 8*(1), 17–18.

Forsyth, Ian. (1998). *"Teaching and Learning Materials and the Internet."* London: Kogan Page.

Forsyth, Ian. (1996). *Teaching and Learning Materials and the Internet.* London: Kogan Page.

Gant, Lenora Peters. (1996, February). "Lessons in Developing Distance Learning." *Performance & Instruction, 35*(2), 22–25.

Garland, Virginia E., and Ann Loranger. (1995-1996). "The Medium and the Message: Interactive Television and Distance Education Programs for Adult Learners." *Journal of Educational Technology Systems, 24*(3), 249–257.

Gibson, Chere Campbell, and Terry L. Gibson. (1997, Winter). "Workshops at a Distance." *New Directions for Adult and Continuing Education, 76,* 59–69.

Goebel, Cathy L. (1998, November). "Web-Based Training, From Soup to Nuts." *Inside Technology Training, 2*(10), 56–61.

Harlamert, Jill A. (1998, Fall). "Effect of Distance Education on Student Learning Methodologies." *Journal of Instruction Delivery Systems, 12*(4), 6–8.

Harlan, Michael R. (1996, Winter). "Corporate Distance Learning Systems for Employee Education." *Journal of Instruction Delivery Systems, 10*(1), 14–16.

"How to Avoid 'Live' Online Training Disasters." (1998, December). *The Microcomputer Trainer, 74,* 5–7.

Hodgson, Pamela. (1999, May). "How to Teach in Cyberspace." *Techniques, 74*(5), 34–36.

Hughes, Chris, and Lindsay Hewson. (1998, July-August). "Online Interactions: Developing a Neglected Aspect of Virtual Classroom." *Educational Technology, 38*(4), 48–55.

Kirk, James J. (1998, November-December). "An Online Webliography." *Technical Training, 9*(6), 4–5.

Koonce, Richard. (1999, January-February). "Stand-up Trainer to Stand-out Facilitator: How to Make the Transition." *Technical Training, 10*(1), 8.

Kruse, Kevin. (1997, February). "Five Levels of Internet-Based Training." *Training & Development, 51*(2), 60–61.

Larson, Matthew R., and Roger Bruning. (1996). "Participant Perceptions of a Collaborative Satellite-Based Mathematics Course. *American Journal of Distance Education, 10*(1), 6–22.

Lawrence, Betty Hurley. (1995-1996). "Teaching and Learning via Video-Conference: The Benefits of Cooperative Learning." *Journal of Educational Technology Systems, 24*(2), 145–149.

Lohmann, Janice Snow. (1998, September). "Classroom Without Walls: Three Companies That Took the Plunge." *Training & Development, 52*(9), 38–41.

Mantyla, Karen, and J. Richard Gividen. *Distance Learning: A Step-by-Step Guide for Trainers.* Alexandria, VA: American Society for Training & Development.

Martinez, Anne. (1998, June). "HP Reaches Out." *Inside Technology Training, 2*(6), 42–45.

Mayadas, A. Frank. (1997, October). "Online Networks Build Time Savings Into Employee Education." *HRMagazine, 42*(10), 31–35.

McIsaac, Marina Stock. (1999). "Distance Learning: The U.S. Version." *Performance Improvement Quarterly, 12*(2), 21–35.

McCormack, Colin, and David Jones. *Building a Web-Based Education System.* New York: John Wiley.

Moller, Leslie. (1998). "Designing Communities of Learners for Asynchronous Distance Education." *Educational Technology Research & Development, 46*(4), 115–122.

Moore, Michael G. (1996). "Media Options." *American Journal of Distance Education, 10*(3), 1–3.

Muldoon, Kathleen. (1996, May-June). "Case Study: Interactive Distance Learning Blooms at Unisys. "*Technical & Skills Training, 7*(4), 28–29.

Munger, Paul David. (1997, January). "High-Tech Training Delivery Methods: When to Use Them." *Training & Development, 51*(1), 46–47.

Oliver, Ron, and Thomas C. Reeves. (1996). "Dimensions of Effective Interactive Learning With Telematics for Distance Education." *Educational Technology Research & Development, 44*(4), 45–56.

Parker, Lorraine. (1996, February). "Make the Most of Teleconferencing." *Training & Development, 50*(2), 28–29.

Patrick, Eric. (1996 Spring). "Distributed Curriculum Development Environments: Techniques and Tools." *Journal of Interactive Instruction Development, 8*(4), 26–34.

Pison, Tom. (1997, August-September). "Distance Learning: Opportunity or Danger?" *Technical Training, 8*(6), 4.

Poppell, Tiffany A. (1998, July). "Training via Videoconferencing." *Training & Development, 52*(7), 15–16.

Pritchard, Carl L. (1998, June). "From Classroom to Chat Room." *Training & Development, 52*(6), 76–77.

Raths, David. (1999, June). "Is Anyone Out There?" *Inside Technology Training, 3*(6), 32–34.

Reneau, Fred W., and Lori L. Kremski-Bronder. (1997, Summer). "Multimedia Integration Into Training Delivered via Desktop Video Conferencing and the Internet." *Journal of Instruction Delivery Systems, 11*(3), 8–14.

Repman, Judi, and Suzanne Logan. (1996 November-December). "Interactions at a Distance: Possible Barriers and Collaborative Solutions." *Techtrends, 41*(6), 35–38.

Schaaf, Dick. (1997, October). "A Pipeline Full of Promises: Distance Training Is Ready to Deliver." *Training, 34,*(10), A6–A22.

Shneiderman, Ben, et al. (1998). "Emergent Patterns of Teaching-Learning in Electronic Classrooms." *Educational Technology Research & Development, 46*(4), 23–42.

Schrum, Lynne. (1998, Summer). "On-Line Education: A Study of Emerging Pedagogy." *New Directions for Adult and Continuing Education, 78*, 53–61.

Schrum, Lynne, and Theodore A. Lamb. (1997, July-August). "Computer Networks as Instructional and Collaborative Distance Learning Environments. *Educational Technology, 37*(4), 26–28.

Shearer, Rick L. (1997). "Classroom Design for Video Teleconferencing." *American Journal of Distance Education, 11*(1), 78–81.

Smith, Constance Ridley. (1996, May). "Taking the Distance out of Distance Learning." *Training & Development, 50*(5), 87–89.

Stewart, James T. (1997, May-June). "Synchronous Distance Learning: The Interactive Internet Classroom." *CBT Solutions,* 25–28.

Thach, Elizabeth C. (1999). "Effective Distance Learning." *Info-line, 9607.* Alexandria, VA: American Society for Training & Development.

Thomerson, J. D., and Clifton L. Smith. (1996). "Student Perceptions of the Affective Experiences Encountered in Distance Learning Courses." *American Journal of Distance Education, 10*(3), 37–48.

Tiene, Drew. (1997, January-February). "Student Perspectives on Distance Learning With Interactive Television." *Techtrends, 42*(1), 41–47.

Trentin, Guglielmo. (1998, May-June). "Computer Conferencing Systems as Seen by a Designer of Online Courses." *Educational Technology, 38*(3), 36–43.

Trentin, Guglielmo, and Vincenza Benigno. (1997, September-October). "Multimedia Conferencing in Education: Methodological and Organizational Considerations." *Educational Technology, 37*(5), 32–39.

Wells, Richard C. (1999, March). "Back to the (Internet) Classroom." *Training, 36(3),* 50–54.

Welsh, Thomas M. (1999, March-April). "Implications of Distributed Learning for Instructional Designers: How Will the Future Affect the Practice?" *Educational Technology, 39*(2), 41–45.

Westbrook, Thomas S. (1997). "Changes in Students' Attitudes Toward Graduate Business Instruction via Interactive Television." *American Journal of Distance Education, 11*(1), 55–69.

Whalen, Tammy, and David Wright. (1999). "Methodology for Cost-Benefit Analysis of Web-Based Telelearning: Case Study of the Bell Online Learning Institute." *American Journal of Distance Education, 13*(1), 24–44.

Wisher, Robert A., and Annette N. Priest. (1998). "Cost-Effectiveness of Audio Teletraining for the U.S. Army National Guard." *American Journal of Distance Education, 12*(1), 38–51.

Wolfe, Thomas E. (1996, Summer). "USAF Initiatives in Distance Learning." *Journal of Instruction Delivery Systems, 10*(3), 12–17.

GENERAL DISTANCE LEARNING BOOKS AND ARTICLES

Abernathy, Donna J. (1998, September). "Distance Learning: Reach Out and Teach Someone." *Training & Development, 52*(9), 28–32.

Ahern, Terence C. (1996, November-December). "A Framework for Improving the Task-to-Technology Fit in Distance Education." *Techtrends, 41*(6), 23–26.

Auerbach, Sarah. (1999, January). "Site Unseen: Keeping Blind Students in Mind Will Make You a Better WBT Designer." *Inside Technology Training, 3*(1), 36–37, 62.

Barron, Ann E. (1996, September-October). "Designing Training for the Web." *Corporate University Review, 4*(5), 24.

Bell, Chris, Mandy Bowden, and Andrew Trott. (1997). *Implementing Flexible Learning.* London: Kogan Page.

Berge, Zane, and Mauri Collins. (1995). *Computer Mediated Communication and the Online Classroom.* Cresskill, NJ: Hampton Press.

Bernstein, Mark. (1998, May). "The Virtual Classroom: A Promising Solution for Teaching Technology." *HRMagazine, 43*(6), 30–33.

Boord, Patricia M. (1998, Winter). "A Distance Learning Case Study." *Journal of Instruction Delivery Systems, 12*(1), 27–35.

Byrne, Bruce S. (1999, January-February). "Distance Learning in Kenya, and the African Virtual University." *Technical Training, 10*(1), 40.

Byrne, Bruce S. (1998, July-August). "Distance Learning: Unrestricted Access." *Technical Training, 9*(4), 14–17.

Calder, Judith, and Ann McCollum. (1998). *Open and Flexible Learning in Vocational Education and Training.* London: Kogan Page.

Care, William Dean. (1996, July-August). "The Transactional Approach to Distance Education." *Adult Learning, 7*(6), 11–12.

Christensen, Kate. (1999). "Case Study: Leveraging Web Technology for Training and Performance Support of Sales Support Staff." *Multimedia & Internet, 5*(11-12), 12–13.

Chute, Alan, Melody Thompson, and Burton Hancock. (1998). *The McGraw-Hill Handbook of Distance Learning.* New York: McGraw-Hill.

Collis, Betty. "Telematics-Supported Education for Traditional Universities in Europe." *Performance Improvement Quarterly, 12*(2), 36–65.

Costello, Bernadette, and Thomas J. Mauter. (1997, May-June). "Going the Distance With (Video) Learning." *Corporate University Review, 5*(3), 10–13.

Crys, Thomas E. (1997). *Teaching at a Distance with the Merging Technologies: An Instructional Systems Approach.* Las Cruces, NM: Center for Educational Development, New Mexico State University.

Dasenbrock, David H. (1996, Summer). "Delivering Distance Learning in a Profit Centered Environment." *Journal of Instruction Delivery Systems, 10*(3), 18–21.

Donoho, Ron. (1998, October). "The New MBA." *Training, 35*(10), DL4–DL9.

Driscoll, Margaret. (1998, November). "How to Pilot Web-Based Training." *Training & Development, 52*(11), 44–49.

Driscoll, Margaret. (1998, July). "Talking to Managers About Web-Based Training." *Multimedia & Internet Training,* 5(7), 6–7.

Dubois, Jacques R. (1996, September-October). "Going the Distance: A National Distance Learning Initiative." *Adult Learning,* 8(1), 19–21.

Duning, Becky, Leon Zabrowski, and Marvin Van Kekerix. (1993). *Reaching Learners through Telecommunications: Management and Leadership Strategies for Higher Education.* San Francisco: Jossey-Bass.

Eastmond, Daniel V. (1998, Summer). "Adult Learners and Internet-Based Distance Education." *New Directions for Adult and Continuing Education,* 33–41.

Ellis, Alan L., Ellen D. Wagner, and Warren R. Longmire. (1999). *Managing Web-Based Training: How to Keep Your Program on Track and Make It Successful.* Alexandria, VA: American Society for Training & Development.

Evans, Terry. (1999). "From Dual-Mode to Flexible Delivery: Paradoxical Transitions in Australian Open and Distance Education." *Performance Improvement Quarterly,* 12(2), 84–95.

Filipczak, Bob. (1997, December). "Are You Wired Enough?" *Training,* 34(12), 34–39.

Filipczak, Bob. (1997, April). "Houston, We Have a Problem." *Training,* 34(4), 56–60.

Filipczak, Bob. (1997, January). "Think Locally, Train Globally." *Training,* 34(1), 40–48.

Filipczak, Bob. (1996, September). "Where Are the Satellites of Yesteryear?" *Training,* 33(9), 73.

Fister, Sarah. (1998, December). "Web-Based Training on a Shoestring." *Training,* 35(12), 42–47.

Fister, Sarah. (1998, November). "The Hybrid Solution: Combining the Web With CD-Rom." *Training,* 35(11), 24–26.

Fryer, Bronwyn. (1999, February). "Beam It Up?" *Inside Technology Training,* 3(2), 36–37.

Fryer, Bronwyn. (1998, October). "MCI Goes Live." *Inside Technology Training,* 2(9), 18–22.

Fryer, Bronwyn. (1997, November). "Better WBT: Beating the Traffic Jam." *Inside Technology Training,* 1(8), 28–31.

Ganzel, Rebecca. (1999, January). "What Price Online Learning?" *Training,* 36(2), 50–54.

Goebel, Cathy L. (1998, November). "Web-Based Training, From Soup to Nuts." *Inside Technology Training,* 2(10), 56–61.

Gordon, Jack. (1997, July). "Infonuggets: The Bite-Sized Future of Corporate Training?" *Training,* 34(7), 26–33.

Hall, Brandon. (1998, July/August). "The Cost of Custom WBT." *Inside Technology Training, 2*(7), 46–47.

Hall, Brandon. (1998, May). "Reeling 'Em in." *Inside Technology Training, 2*(5), 34–36.

Hall, Brandon. (1997). *Web-Based Training Cookbook.* New York: John Wiley.

Harasim, Linda, Starr Roxanne Hiltz, Lucio Teles, and Murray Turoff. (1995). *Learning Networks: A Field Guide to Teaching and Learning Online.* Cambridge, MA: MIT Press.

Harlamert, Jill A. (1998, Fall). "Effect of Distance Education on Student Learning Methodologies." *Journal of Instruction Delivery Systems, 12*(4), 6–8.

Hartnett, John. (1999, January). "The Best Laid Plans of WBT." *Inside Technology Training, 3*(1), 38–40.

Hawkridge, David. (1999). "Distance Learning: International Comparisons." *Performance Improvement Quarterly, 12*(2), 9–20.

Hettinger, James. (1997, October). "Degree by E-mail." *Techniques, 72*(7), 21–23.

Hickman, Clark J. (1999, Spring). "Public Policy Implications Associated With Technology Assisted Distance Learning." *Adult Learning, 10*(3), 17–20.

Hopey, Christopher E., and Lynda Ginsburg. (1996, September-October). "Distance Learning and New Technologies: You Can't Predict the Future, but You Can Plan for It." *Adult Learning, 8*(1), 22–23.

Jayasinghe, Mala Gopalakrishnan, Gary R. Morrison, and Steven M. Ross. (1997). "The Effect of Distance Learning Classroom Design on Student Perceptions." *Educational Technology Research & Development, 45*(4), 5–19.

"JCPenney Embraces Distance Learning." (1998, May-June). *Corporate University Review, 6*(3), 42–44.

Johnson, Dan F. (1996, Summer). "Will My Visuals Work on My Video Distance Learning System?" *Journal of Interactive Instruction Development, 9*(1), 22–25.

Jossi, Frank. (1998, October). "Videoconferencing on the Cheap." *Training, 35*(10), DL10–DL20.

Kasten, Paul. (1998, January-February). "Customer Service Training: Within Budget." *Technical Training, 9*(1), 20–22.

Keast, David A. (1997). "Toward an Effective Model for Implementing Distance Education Programs." *American Journal of Distance Education, 11*(2), 39–55.

Keizer, Gregg. (1999, April). "Seeing Eye to Eye." *Inside Technology Training, 3*(4), 42–45.

Kemper, Cynthia L. (1998, November-December). "Web-Based Training Comes of Age." *Technical Training, 9*(6), 6–7.

Kenyon, Henry. (1999, March-April). "How Do You Train Two Million People? Manpower's Answer Is 'Log on.'" *Corporate University Review, 7*(2), 24–27.

Kenyon, Henry S. (1998, November-December). "New Twists on Management, Professional Training: Universities Team With Online Learning Providers." *Corporate University Review, 6*(6), 31–32.

Kenyon, Henry S. (1998, January-February). "Growth of BTV Is Talk of Telecon Confab." *Corporate University Review, 6*(1), 31–33.

Kiernan, Terry. (1998, June). "Providing Direction in Web-Based Training: Guidelines for Designing Navigation." *Multimedia & Internet Training, 5*(6), 6.

King, Kathleen P. (1998, Summer). "Course Development on the World Wide Web." *New Directions for Adult and Continuing Education,* 25–32.

Kirk, James J. (1998, March-April). "Online Web-Based Training Resources." *Technical Training, 9*(2), 4–5.

Krebs, Arlene. (1996). *The Distance Learning Funding Sourcebook: A Guide to Foundation, Corporate and Government Support for Telecommunications and the New Media.* Dubuque, IA: Kendall/Hunt Publishing Company.

Kremer, D. (1996). *Accelerating Change.* Littleton, CO: Virginia Ostendorf, Inc.

Laney, James D. (1996, March-April). "Going the Distance: Effective Instruction Using Distance Learning Technology." *Educational Technology, 36*(2), 51–54.

Latchem, Colin, Szarina Abdullah, and Ding Xingfu. (1999). "Open and Dual-Mode Universities in East and South Asia. *Performance Improvement Quarterly, 12*(2), 96–121.

Lee, Andrea J., and Tracy G. Marsh. (1998). "Joint Ventures in Distance Education: Mapping Uncharted Domain." *American Journal of Distance Education, 12*(2), 54–62.

Lozada, Marlene. (1997, October). "Look out for Distance Learning." *Techniques, 72*(7), 24–26.

Magalhaes, Monica G.M., and Dietrich Schiel. (1997). "A Method for Evaluation of a Course Delivered via the World Wide Web in Brazil." *American Journal of Distance Education, 11*(2), 64–70.

Martin, Merle, and Stanley A. Taylor. (1997, September-October). "The Virtual Classroom: The Next Steps." *Educational Technology, 37*(5), 51–55.

Marx, Raymond J. (1999). *The ASTD Media Selection Tool for Workplace Learning.* Alexandria, VA: American Society for Training & Development.

McVay, M. (1998). *How to Be a Successful Distance Student: Learning on the Internet.* Needham Heights, MA: Simon & Schuster.

Miller, Inabeth, and Jeremy Schlosberg. (1997). *Kaplan Guide to Distance Learning.* New York: Kaplan Books.

Moore, Michael G. (1996). "Tips for the Manager Setting up a Distance Education Program." *American Journal of Distance Education, 10*(1), 1–5.

Moshinskie, James F. (1997, Winter). "The Effects of Using Constructivist Learning Models When Delivering Electronic Distance Education (EDE) Courses: A Perspective Study." *Journal of Instruction Delivery Systems, 11*(1), 14–20.

Murphy, Kate. (1999, April 5). "Welcome to the World of MBA.com." *Business Week,* 120.

Panepinto, Joe. (1999, April). "A Meeting of the Minds." *Inside Technology Training, 3*(4), 16–19.

Pantazis, Cynthia. (1998, July-August). "Training Through Collaboration: Michigan Virtual Automotive College." *Technical Training, 9*(4), 29–31.

Pastore, Raymond S. (1998, February). "Strategies for Translating Classroom Instruction to Web-Based Courses." *Multimedia & Internet Training, 5*(2), 6–7.

Phillips, Vicky. (1998, July). "Online Universities Teach Knowledge Beyond the Books." *HRMagazine, 43*(8), 120–128.

Phillips, Vicky. (1998, May). "Virtual Classrooms, Real Education." *Nation's Business, 86*(5), 41–45.

Piskurich, George and Ethan Sanders. (1998). *ASTD Models for Learning Technologies: Roles, Competencies, and Outputs.* Alexandria, VA: American Society for Training & Development.

Piskurich, George. (1993). *The ASTD Handbook of Instructional Technology.* New York: McGraw-Hill.

Poley, Janet K. (1998). "Creating Shared Leadership Environments in Institutional and International Settings." *American Journal of Distance Education, 12*(2), 16–25.

Porter, Lynette R. (1997). *Creating the Virtual Classroom: Distance Learning with the Internet.* New York: John Wiley.

Porter, Patrick. (1999, March). "Boeing's Big Experiment." *Inside Technology Training, 3*(3), S8–S12.

Quinlan, Laurie R. (1996, November-December). "The Digital Classroom." *Techtrends, 41*(6), 6–8.

Rayl, Karen. (1998, April). "GTE's Training Goes High-Tech." *Workforce, 77*(4), 36–40.

Repman, Judi, and Suzanne Logan. (1996, November-December). "Interactions at a Distance: Possible Barriers and Collaborative Solutions." *Techtrends, 41*(6), 35–38.

Roberts, Bill. (1998, August). "Training via the Desktop." *HRMagazine, 43*(9), 98–104.

Rumble, Greville. (1999). "Cost Analysis of Distance Learning." *Performance Improvement Quarterly, 12*(2), 122–137.

Rumble, Greville. (1997). *The Costs and Economics of Open and Distance Learning.* London: Kogan Page.

Russell, T.L. (1999). *The No Significant Difference Phenomenon.* Raleigh, NC: North Carolina State University.

Sachs, Steven G. (1999). "The Mature Distance Education Program— Which Way Now?" *Performance Improvement Quarterly, 12*(2), 66–83.

Saltzman, Phyllis. (1997). "The Learning Council: Corporate Distance Learning in Action." *American Journal of Distance Education, 11*(2), 56–63.

Schreiber, Deborah and Zane L. Berge. (1998). *Distance Training: How Innovative Organizations are Using Technology to Maximize Learning and Meet Business Objectives.* San Francisco: Jossey-Bass.

Shotsberger, Paul G. (1996, March-April). "Instructional Uses of the World Wide Web: Exemplars and Precautions." *Educational Technology, 36*(2), 47–50.

Simonson, Michael, Charles Schlosser, and Dan Hanson. (1999). "Theory and Distance Education: A New Discussion." *American Journal of Distance Education, 13*(1) 60–75.

Smith, Thomas W. (1998). "Distance Education Is a Strategy: What Is the Objective?" *American Journal of Distance Education, 12*(2), 63–72.

Snell, Ned. (1999, May). "We Reveal the Cost of WBT." *Inside Technology Training, 3*(5), 13–15.

Spitzer, Dean R. (1998, March-April). "Rediscovering the Social Context of Distance Learning." *Educational Technology, 38*(2), 52–56.

Stansbury, Ray. (1996 November-December). "Copyright and Distance Learning: A Balancing Act." *Techtrends, 41*(6), 9–11.

Starner, Tom. (1999, March 4). "Cyber Schools." *Human Resource Executive, 13*(3), 30–36.

Starr, Robin M. (1997, May-June). "Delivering Instruction on the World Wide Web: Overview and Basic Design Principles." *Educational Technology, 37*(3), 7–15.

Stone, David E., and Clarke A. Bishop. (1997, Fall). "Web-Based Training: How to Really Do It." *Journal of Instruction Delivery Systems, 11*(4), 3–9.

Stone, Nigel, and Ian Williams. (1996, Fall). "Supported Distance Learning as an O.D. Intervention." *Organization Development Journal, 14*(3), 71–78.

Theibert, Philip R. (1996, February). "Train and Degree Them—Anywhere." *Personnel Journal, 75*(2), 28–37.

Ubois, Jeff. (1999, April). "Help Wanted: Distance Learning Director." *Inside Technology Training, 3*(4), 32–33.

"Unique Combination of Satellite TV, Gamesmanship Improves Ethics Training." (1997, January). *Training Directors' Forum Newsletter, 13*(1), 5.

Ward, Douglas R., and Esther L. Tiessen. (1997, September-October). "Adding Educational Value to the Web: Active Learning With AlivePages." *Educational Technology, 37*(5), 22–31.

Welch, Jim. (1998, June 25). "Happy Campus?" *People Management, 4*(13), 46–50.

Williams, Deborah, and Scott Stahl. (1996, November-December). "Ford's Lessons in Distance Learning." *Technical & Skills Training, 7*(8), 10–13.

Williams, Russ. (1998, June). "Modems and Response Times: How to Design for Optimal Web Training." *Multimedia & Internet Training, 5*(6), 4–5.

Willis, Barry. (1998, January-February). "Effective Distance Education Planning: Lessons Learned." *Educational Technology, 38*(1), 57–59.

Willis, Barry. (1994). *Distance Education: Strategies and Tools.* Englewood Cliffs, NJ: Educational Technology Publications.

Yong, Yanyan. (1998, Winter). "Learners' Perceptions on Learning Through the Web." *Journal of Instruction Delivery Systems, 12*(1), 23–26.

OTHER PERIODICALS ON DISTANCE LEARNING

The American Journal of Distance Education
Tel: 814.863.3784
http://www.ed.psu.edu/ACSDE

DEOSNEWS
To subscribe to this online newsletter, post the following command to
LISTSERV@LISTS.PSU.EDU
SUBSCRIBE DEOSNEWS skip one space, and type your
First and Last names.

The Distance Education Report
Magna Publications
Tel: 800.433.0499
Email: custserv@magnapubs.com

Multimedia & Internet Training Newsletter
Email: editor@brandon-hall.com

University Access: A Quarterly Online Journal Devoted to Distance Learning
Tel: 877.932.9400
http://www.academyonline.com

Inside Technology Training
Tel: 888.950.4302
http://www.ittrain.com

DISTANCE LEARNING RESOURCES ON THE WORLD WIDE WEB

These online references are from the World Wide Web and include the appropriate URL address. Please keep in mind that in the future, some of these sites might move or be discontinued.

American Center for the Study of Distance Education
http://www.ed.psu.edu/ACSDE

American Society for Training & Development
http://www.astd.org/virtual_community

Arizona State University
Distance Learning Technology
http://www-distlearn.pp.asu.edu

AT&T Learning Network®
http://www.att.com/learningnetwork

Blackboard.com
http://www.blackboard.com

Distance Education and Training Council
http://www.detc.org

Distance Learning Consultants
http://www.geteducated.com

The Masie Center
http://www.masie.com

PBS Business Channel
Adult Learning Resources for Learners
http://pbs.org/adultlearning

Training Super Site
http://www.trainingsupersite.com

University Access
http://www.universityaccess.com

University of Idaho
Distance Education at a Glance
http://www.uidaho.edu/evo/distglan.html

University of Maryland System
Institute for Distance Education and the
International University Consortium
http://www2.ncsu.edu/ncsu/cc/pub/teachtools/ConfReport.htm

University of Wisconsin
Distance Education Clearinghouse
http://www.uwex.edu/disted/home.html

U.S. Distance Learning Association
http://www.usdla.org

Dedication

I would like to dedicate this book to:

My mother, Sylvia Fischer, who at 87 years young, has been my lifetime cheerleader and role model in always doing your best and doing whatever it takes to maintain a positive attitude.

My son, Michael, who reflects all that a parent hopes for in helping to develop an outstanding and caring person. His constant stretch for excellence, resulting achievements, and dedication to public service are always a source of inspiration for me.

My personal life partner, Bob Engelhardt, who urged me to write this book when ASTD contacted me, who supports what I do and how I do it, and who is an excellent trainer.

And to Brittany, Bob's 13-year-old daughter, who endured the pain of listening to LOW-volume music so that I could work at home. Thanks Britt.

About the Author

Karen Mantyla is president of Quiet Power, Inc., a distance learning training and consulting company in Washington, D.C. She received her professional certification in distance learning from the University of Wisconsin-Madison, a renowned leader in distance education. She is the co-author of the book *Distance Learning: A Step-by-Step Guide for Trainers,* published by the American Society for Training & Development in 1997, and *Consultative Sales Power,* published by Crisp Publications in 1995. *The 2000 ASTD Distance Learning Handbook* will be available from McGraw-Hill early in 2000.

Mantyla serves as an active team member of both the Technology and Communications Committees of the Federal Government Distance Learning Association (FGDLA). She is the editor of *Distance Learning News,* the official publication of the Federal Government Distance Learning Association, a specialized chapter of the United States Distance Learning Association (USDLA). She is an active member of the American Society for Training & Development (ASTD) and is a certified facilitator for the Human Performance Improvement Certification Program offered by ASTD. She consults with both public- and private-sector clients to help design, develop, implement, and maintain distance learning systems. Her focus is on the human side of the distance learning equation to ensure that trainers receive proper support, guidance, and training in selecting and utilizing distance learning methods of delivery. In addition, she helps design learner support systems, tools, and methods to ensure success and continuous process improvement for all remote site facilitators and learners.

Mantyla has more than 15 years of specialized experience in the development and implementation of workplace education programs, with specific emphasis on reaching learners in dispersed geographic locations. She has held many senior leadership positions, including vice presidency of a *Fortune* 500 corporation. Her biography is featured in the 2000 edition of *Who's Who in the World, Who's Who in America, Who's Who of American Women,* and *Who's Who in Finance and Industry.* Her plans include writing and designing additional multimedia resources to help trainers and their organizations achieve distance learning success in the 21st century.